September 1997

A side trip to Savannah from Hilton Head

SAVANNAH ENTERTAINS

MARTHA GIDDENS NESBIT

Wyrick & Company

Published by Wyrick & Company
1-A Pinckney Street
Charleston, S.C. 29401

Designed by Sally Heineman
Printed and bound in Hong Kong

Library of Congress Cataloging-in-Publication Data

Nesbit, Martha Giddens.
Savannah entertains / by Martha Nesbit.
p. cm.
Includes bibliographical references and index.
ISBN 0-941711-35-8 (alk. paper)
1. Cookery. American--Southern style. 2. Cookery--Georgia--
Savannah. 3. Entertaining. 4. Menus. I. Title.
TX715.2.S68N47 1996
641.59758'724--dc20   96-17660

Photo Credits: Party photographs are by Steve Bisson,
with two exceptions: Elizabeth Terry's Tybee Porch Supper,
by Charlie Ribbens; Thanksgiving Feast by Paula Williamson.
Food Styling by Don Bass.

CONTENTS

PREFACE

My introduction to Savannah entertaining occurred in 1974. I was four months out of college, new to Savannah and marveling at the good fortune of having secured a coveted job in the Women's News department of the *Savannah Morning News and Evening Press*, Savannah's daily newspaper.

My future husband, Gary, lived on the ground floor of a historic townhouse owned by a delightful lady named Sally Sullivan. Not long after our meeting, Mrs. Sullivan issued an invitation to a small cocktail party she was having in honor of her daughter, Sarah Armstrong, who was visiting from Raleigh. Mrs. Sullivan explained that she was having a few old friends in for drinks, and she'd like for us to meet them.

Mrs. Sullivan's little party was the first taste I had of how Savannah entertains. The ripe tomato sandwiches with homemade onion mayonnaise and the oysters in cream sauce spooned from an heirloom chafing dish and served in toast cups made it clear to me from the beginning that Savannah's culinary style was something special.

Much of that evening was spent with "natives"— people Savannah-born and Savannah-bred—politely but pointedly inquiring as to my origins. "Are you a native?" they asked. No, I was from Valdosta, Georgia. "Are any of your people from Savannah?" they wondered. The fact that my mother was a Lane from nearby Statesboro with distant ties to a prominent family in the city seemed to justify further

inquiry as to other important topics—my schooling (a satisfactory state college), job aspirations (journalism seemed acceptable), apartment location (in the historic district, thank goodness) and, finally, church affiliation (not Episcopalian, but at least I was an attending Methodist).

It was an exciting, if exhausting, evening.

Mrs. Sullivan, as it turned out, was the premiere caterer of her time, dishing up delectables at party after party to a loyal clientele she described as "the loveliest people in town." When Gary and I met her, she was 82, and greeted us on every visit perfectly coiffed, dressed in a shirtwaist dress, stockings and sensible pumps, since she did not drive and was constantly on foot. Even in pumps, she was less than 5 feet tall, with twinkling eyes and deep dimples. Mrs. Sullivan was blessed with an amazing energy and a lively wit. She was also a fabulous cook, having built her catering reputation on fresh seafood in every form, sophisticated casseroles and country ham. We became good friends.

In her front parlor, Mrs. Sullivan would entertain us with stories of parties, party food and partygoers, often telling the same tales over and over again in the same manner while we pretended we had never heard any of it before.

It was Mrs. Sullivan, then, who first sparked my interest in Savannah parties, and it is to the memory of Mrs. Sullivan—who died in 1989 at age 95—that this book is primarily dedicated. Her Rice Krispy cheese biscuits—delivered with great fanfare in a small rectangular cardboard box each Christmas, accompanied by a new tea towel—will always be fondly remembered. (The recipe can be found in our Thanksgiving Feast menu.)

This book is dedicated as well to all the caterers and good cooks—many of whom are featured in this collection—who followed in Mrs. Sullivan's steady footsteps. These cooks can be credited with continuing the great Savannah tradition of serving regional ingredients, simply prepared and elegantly turned out. Those of us who enjoy Savannah's unique culinary style today are the beneficiaries of their good taste.

ACKNOWLEDGEMENTS

In the winter of 1992, I asked Steve Bisson, a photographer I had known for more than a decade at the *Savannah News-Press*, if he would be interested in shooting photographs for a book I had in mind on Savannah entertaining. Without hesitation (and with little apparent concern about who we would get to publish such a book), Steve said "yes." Steve photographed all but two of the parties (he was ill both times). We were grateful that Charlie Ribbens and Paula Williamson could step in at the last minute.

Not long after approaching Steve, I mentioned the book to stylist Don Bass, asking if he, too, would like to participate on this long-ranged, not-exactly-a-sure-thing project. Like Steve, Don gave an enthusiastic, "Sure!" So, for more than three years, we have worked together as a team, lugging food and props, styling, tilting dishes with wallets, tasting and sometimes worrying. I want to thank Don and Steve for believing that I could eventually put this book together.

Later, another gentleman would also become important in this project: publisher Pete Wyrick, too, felt this was an idea worth developing. For his faith in our idea and attention to detail, I wish to say thank you, as well as to the rest of the staff at Wyrick & Company.

Others lending moral support along the way include caterer Trish McLeod, who kept saying, "Martha, just do it!" and bookseller Esther Shaver, who knows more about this business than just about anyone I've met, and graciously offered advice when it was needed. My friends Dottie Courington and Beth Taylor proofread the initial manuscript and helped reshape the book's content. Your support kept me plugging away, even when I felt the project was too big to finish. My walking buddies—Wez, Lynn and Jenny—offered wise counsel and listening ears.

Special thanks are owed to all the hosts, hostesses and cooks who are credited elsewhere. They opened their homes, kitchens and recipe books to me, Don and Steve, allowing us to plunder for just the right cracked bowl or silver oyster fork to use in our photographs. We were always treated with warm smiles and the graciousness and hospitality that Savannah is known for. Thank you, all.

My appreciation of good-tasting, simple food was formed through the years at the family dinner table, eating the down-home creations of my grandmother, Mary Lane, mother, Alice Jo Giddens, aunts Betty Lane and Sue Lane, and in-laws Tom and Mona Nesbit. They showed me how to set a table with the best we had, decorate with whatever was growing in the yard and prepare whatever dishes would most please our guests, no matter how much trouble was required to prepare them. I will never forget.

Behind the scenes—tasting, cooking, hauling, waiting, questioning and, occasionally needling and chiding—was my family: husband, Gary, and boys Zack and Emory. I love you better than ice cream.

INTRODUCTION

Without question, Savannahians entertain with great personal style. Take, for example, this simple lunch for two. I was a young reporter, invited to a grand turn of the century mansion by a seasoned female journalist who wanted to show me the ropes. I was greeted by the family's uniformed butler, and, after a tour of the house (including the closets!), was seated with my hostess at a massive mahogany dining table set with scalloped linen placemats, embroidered linen napkins and heavy silver engraved with the family initial. The first course was new to me—a single, giant Vidalia onion, baked whole and oozing butter. I have experienced many innovative appetizers since, but few more memorable that that onion, served with great flourish on the family china by the most personable of butlers. Chalk one up for Savannah style.

If an intimate luncheon is cause for setting the finest table, you can imagine what Savannah does when the occasion calls for a big celebration. There are debutante parties with elaborate, themed food stations set underneath ballroom-sized

tents; wedding receptions with several hundred guests clustered along the lawn of a waterfront home or standing shoulder to shoulder in the gallery of the local art museum, feasting on more than a dozen local specialties, from oysters on the half shell and frozen vodka to baked quail and buttery shrimp; bridge luncheons for 48 matrons where ice water is served in silver goblets, potent toddies are passed, and starched white linen tablecloths are spread in readiness for dainty portions of some delicious regional dish.

Not all of the best parties are formal affairs, however. Savannahians, in fact, take pride in the fact that some of their most successful gatherings center around mud and gnats.

In the winter, there are oyster roasts, messy affairs where old jeans, a warm jacket, a hearty appetite for bivalves and congenial conversation with your oyster-shucking neighbors are the rules of thumb. During the late summer and early fall, an eagerly anticipated event is the Lowcountry Boil, when shrimp are plentiful, corn is at perfection and sand gnats and mosquitoes compete for nibbles of the guests' exposed skin. There are also, for a lucky few, picnics on one of the wild barrier islands, such as Ossabaw or Wassaw, an hour or so by boat from one of Savannah's many marinas. There, away from any influence but nature, picnickers can watch the marine ecosystem at work—egrets catching shrimp, pelicans diving for fish and bottlenose dolphin playing in the Atlantic waters.

Savannahians tend to celebrate just about anything—births, christenings, graduations, holidays, new friends, new jobs, personal accomplishments, even new rugs! Just after we moved to Isle of Hope, a sleepy island community just minutes from the outskirts of Savannah, two dear ladies had me in for an old-fashioned, new-neighbor tea. About 75 islanders showed up to greet me, and we enjoyed bite-sized tea sandwiches, platters of fruit and sweets, and plenty of wine in the middle of the afternoon. Savannahians need little prompting to throw a party!

ESSENTIAL ELEMENTS

Savannah caterer Susan Mason is confident that "No place entertains quite like Savannah. I'm not sure whether people here have an innate love of good food, or it's because we're on the coast and have so much to work with. Regardless, our parties are really special. Savannahians like to use their pretty things, and they are great collectors. And they love to entertain at home."

Savannahians do, indeed, love a home party. "Home" might be an antique-filled downtown townhouse, a traditional two-story columned home in midtown, a Lowcountry bungalow overlooking the marsh, a hunting plantation in the woods, or a modern, airy mansion set in an island community.

No matter where "home" is, count on Savannah entertainers to use the scenery to maximum advantage. Outdoor wedding receptions are planned when the white dogwood and fuschia azaleas are in contrasting bloom. Cocktail parties are arranged to show off the Lady Banks Rose or the fragrant Indian Hawthorne. Seafood parties are scheduled when the moon is full and the tide is high enough to stir the gnats.

Proper presentation is a detail Savannahians relish. Party-givers decorate their mantels and platters with whatever is lush and native plucked from the yard—moss, ivy, camellias, azaleas, hydrangeas and palmetto fronds, for example. Savannah hostesses are particularly fond of the magnolia, which offers leaves, blossoms and seed cones to display.

One older Savannah hostess told me once that she had never bought a paper plate. "Even when I pack a picnic for my grandchildren, I like to use the good china," she said sweetly. Likewise, Savannahians are apt to take silver to a picnic in the park. They don't consider this showing off, but sharing the best they have with the people they cherish, whether family or friends.

But far and above, the most essential elements to a Savannah party are the warm hospitality one will experience and the entertaining conversations one is apt to hear from people who pride themselves on being unconventional. The best Savannah hosts and hostesses have an uncanny way of mixing old and new residents, guests from several generations, and friends from all walks of life.

Arthur Gordon, author, former magazine editor,

native Savannahian and nephew of Girl Scouts founder Juliette Gordon Low, gives this apt appraisal of the Savannah character: "Savannahians are good story tellers, great raconteurs. We have a droll sense of humor. You go to dinner parties, and you may as well be at the theater. We mostly have good manners and tend to value them more than other people do. For generations, it was more important to have good manners than money because there wasn't any money to be had. We are a proud people, and we have a lot to be proud of. But we occasionally take offense too easily." Such characteristics make for lively parties.

The Savannah guest is never allowed to be ill at ease. We were young and inexperienced on the dinner party circuit when my husband and I were invited to dine at the home of a museum director and his wife. When we arrived, our host opened the door, and, seeing that my husband was tieless, announced: "Oh, goody. You decided not to wear a tie." He ripped the silk ascot from his neck and ushered us in with great fanfare. This effort to make each guest feel comfortable is graciousness at its best, and graciousness is an art Savannah hosts and hostesses have cultivated to perfection.

The settings, the presentation, and Savannah hospitality serve to enhance the final ingredients essential to any Savannah party—glorious food and plenty of good drink.

INGREDIENTS AND CULINARY STYLE

The cooking that has survived in Savannah's finest kitchens is a result of who we are, where we live, what we had to cook with and who was in the kitchen doing the cooking. There are several excellent resources that elaborate more fully on the cuisine of our region, but this section is meant as a quick overview, and is mostly my opinion, formed from hours thumbing through journals at the Georgia Historical Society and reading the sources mentioned in the bibliography.

Savannahians are, of course, part of the Deep South, and share the appreciation all Southern cooks have for food harvested at its peak. Ears of silver queen corn are picked when the kernels are the size of a baby tooth and so full of milk that they burst at the slightest pressure. Okra is snapped off the bush when it's the size of a pinkie. Tomatoes are pulled when the color has turned a particular shade of ruby. Fresh vegetables, picked at their peak and cooked with nothing but a little water and smoked meat for seasoning, sopped up with cornbread or biscuits, was a meal that helped farm families through tough times.

Savannahians still cook by the seasons. We eagerly await the first Vidalia onions in May, peaches and peanuts in June and July, Atlantic blue crabs in late summer and scuppernongs by Labor Day.

There is ample evidence that Southerners have always had a healthy supply of produce to choose from. A description of a Georgia garden in the 1850s mentions scuppernong grapes, asparagus and strawberry beds, raspberries, artichokes, beans, peas, okra, tomatoes, cucumbers, lettuces, potatoes, turnips, watermelon and a wide variety of herbs—sage, sweet basil, thyme, sweet marjoram, coriander, horseradish, leeks, onions and garlic.

Rice in the South was often eaten twice a day. Corn was dried and ground into hominy, grits and cornmeal. Biscuits, cornbread, yeast rolls and hushpuppies are Southern breads that have retained their popularity through the centuries. Some things cannot be improved upon.

Southern bounty also included wild game—the woods provided deer, turkey, quail, duck and doves. Pork, however, was the most prominent meat on the Southern table for many years.

The Lowcountry culinary heritage adds to all of the above the abundance of the sea—primarily shrimp, oysters, fish and crab. Diamondback terrapin, canvasback duck and boned shad were three epicurean delights of the past. Accounts of life at summer houses in the late 1800s describe fishing, rowing, crabbing and berry-picking as favorite activities. Entertaining was casual according to one hostess, who often had 8 to 14 at her table. "We live chiefly from what the waters furnish and vegetables of which we get a full supply."

From the first days, Native Americans taught Georgia's colonists how to hunt and fish, gather honey, roast oysters and grow and use corn. Because Savannah was a thriving port city, residents had all that was provided by land and sea, as well as an almost unlimited assortment of edibles that arrived from European ports.

The English colonists brought with them their taste for cream sauces and their English cookery books. But the cooks in most English homes were African, and those cooks added their own exotic seasonings and culinary techniques that resulted in dishes such as oyster pilau and okra and tomatoes. What happened when these three forces joined—the meeting of native ingredients, English tastebuds and African culinary skill—created the magic that exemplifies Savannah's finest cooking today.

Some of Savannah's favorite desserts illustrate how the three influences can coexist. A city with a pronounced sweet tooth, Savannahians love everything from the classically Southern caramel layer cake to the custard-based English cream caramel to the decidedly African-influenced benne seed cookie.

Always in Savannah, good food is washed down with good drink. The oft-repeated saying is that if you go to Atlanta, people want to know your line of work. In Macon, they ask where you go to church. In Savannah, you are sure to be asked "What do you like to drink?" In the 18th and 19th centuries, affluent Georgians brought in wines from Madeira, the Canary Islands, France and Spain. A Madeira Club still exists, where wines are featured at formal dinners and club members hear a paper on a timely topic, delivered by one of their group. Martinis, iced champagne, fine wine, Bloody Marys and Mint Juleps are libations Savannahians hold dear.

A drink rarely served but often written about is Chatham Artillery Punch (see recipe on page 121), a sneaky concoction made with hefty portions of brandy, whiskey, rum and champagne, their kick camouflaged by green tea, lemon and sugar. The drink dates back to the 1850s. I've only been served it twice in 20 years, both times in frosted pewter mugs. I don't remember much else about either evening!

ABOUT THIS BOOK

This book contains typical Savannah dishes served in appropriate settings, following the seasons for culinary and decorative ideas. Just which parties to include and what recipes to share are purely the author's choice. This book is not intended to be a historical account of the way Savannah entertained in the past, nor does it seek to duplicate historical recipes. It is a modern book, designed for modern cooks, modern timetables, modern budgets and modern tastes.

Although Southerners, like cooks in the rest of the country, have modified their habits in recent years to reduce fat in everyday meals, this book was designed for special occasions, when flavor should win out over fat count. Butter, cream and cheese often mean the difference between so-so and delicious. Feel free to make the customary low-fat substitutions if you are serious about fat grams, but do be prepared for changes in flavor and consistency.

This book is foremost a cookbook, meaning that the recipes are the most important element. The food, I believed, needed to reflect Savannah's long-standing tradition of good food, simply made and presented well.

Many of the recipes were provided by reliable sources, who are credited elsewhere. Others are original recipes, created specifically for this collection. All were tested to make sure they would work in your kitchen. While every effort was made to keep recipes free of canned or processed products, there is an occasional convenience product or brand name called for if I felt it was in the best interest of the finished dish.

Because some of the parties are quite elaborate, cooks may want to do ahead as much of the menu as possible. Therefore, I have noted which dishes freeze particularly well.

Finally, a note about the way this book is put together.

Every party lists the complete menu and provides the recipes. Photographs document each set-ting and show how some of the completed dishes should look. Indigenous flowers, herbs and greenery were used to garnish, in the event you want to duplicate the dish exactly.

Savannah continues its rich tradition of giving parties, each one different in menu, decor, setting and overall ambience. It is this great variety in style and flavors I have tried to capture through photographs and recipes. May you have the best of luck in creating your own celebrations!

Martha Nesbit
February, 1996

NEW YEAR'S DAY GOOD LUCK MEAL

Just about anyone who has been to Savannah has heard of Mrs. Wilkes' Boarding House restaurant. Sema Wilkes and her husband L.H. have run the boarding house and restaurant, located on a quiet street in the historic district of downtown Savannah, since the 1940s.

The boarding house never advertises, but people from around the world find the dining room all the same. Once they do, they sit at round tables and serve themselves family-style from platters and serving bowls piled high with favorites like black-eyed peas, turnip greens, macaroni and cheese and fried chicken with cornbread dressing. Mrs. Wilkes' style of cooking is traditionally Southern, relying on the use of vegetables straight from the fields, often seasoned with a piece of smoked ham hock. Nobody cooks Southern vegetables better than Mrs. Wilkes.

That's why we thought of her when planning our good luck meal, typically eaten sometime on New Year's Day. (Some folks get a jump on things and serve themselves at midnight New Year's Eve!) The greens ensure good cash flow, the peas are for good luck, the pork is for prosperity, and the cornbread is included to sop up all that delicious "pot likker" from the greens. Chowchow—a relish made with peppers and often including corn—and pepper vinegar to dribble on the peas and greens—are traditional accompaniments. We always eat this meal with a tall glass of iced tea, even in winter. Plan to serve the pecan pie later in the day with a pot of hot coffee.

MENU

•

TURNIP GREENS

HOPPIN' JOHN

ROAST PORK

CORNBREAD MUFFINS

SOUTHERN SWEET TEA

PECAN PIE

TURNIP GREENS

1 bunch fresh turnip greens
1 medium piece salt pork
2 cups water
1 teaspoon salt
2 tablespoons butter or
  margarine, optional

Strip leaves from stems. Wash thoroughly, in several changes of water. Place leaves in large heavy-bottomed saucepan. Add salt pork, water and salt. Cook at medium heat for several minutes, then reduce heat to low, cover, and cook for about 45 minutes, until tender. Remove pork. Shred greens with two knives, used scissor-fashion. Taste and add more salt if necessary. There will be a small amount of liquid, which is called pot liquor. Serve it with the cornbread. Add 2 tablespoons butter or margarine to greens before serving, if desired.

Serves 6 to 8.

HOPPIN' JOHN

1½ cups dried cow peas, or black-eyed peas, soaked
1 cup celery, chopped
2 medium onions, chopped
1 medium green pepper, chopped
2 small ham hocks, or a large meaty ham bone
Salt and pepper to taste
1 cup rice, approximately
Minced onion
Minced green pepper

Combine everything but rice in heavy pot. Cover peas with water and cook until peas are done, about 2 to 3 hours. Continue to add small amounts of water if peas appear too dry. Remove ham hock or bone, pick meat from bone and return to pot, if desired.

Prepare rice separately and serve peas over rice, with minced onion and green pepper, if desired.

Or, for a one-pot dish, fold in raw rice, the amount depending on the amount of liquid you have in the peas. (A guide is 1 cup rice to 2 cups liquid. You may have to add a little water to make sure you have enough liquid to cook rice.) Cook about 25 minutes, until rice is tender.

Serves 6 to 8. Freezes well. Let thaw in refrigerator and reheat. You may need to add a little water while reheating.

ROAST PORK

1 4- to 5-pound pork tenderloin
1 teaspoon salt
1 teaspoon pepper
1 teaspoon paprika
2 cups water

Combine dry ingredients. Sprinkle evenly over pork roast. Place roast in roaster; add water. Seal top of roaster with foil. Bake at 350° for 2 hours or more, until pork roast is very tender and no pink remains.

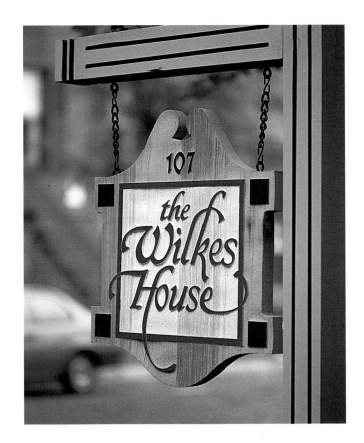

CORNBREAD MUFFINS

2 cups self-rising cornmeal
1¹/₂ cups buttermilk
¹/₄ teaspoon baking soda
1 egg
3 tablespoons bacon grease

Dissolve baking soda in buttermilk. Make a well in cornmeal. Combine buttermilk, egg and bacon grease. Mix well. Pour liquids all at once into cornmeal and mix quickly.

Fill well-greased muffin tins three-quarters full. Bake at 450° for 20 minutes.

Makes 12 muffins.

SOUTHERN SWEET TEA

1 quart water
7 small tea bags
1 cup sugar

Bring water to boil in heavy tea kettle. Turn off heat, add tea bags, place lid on kettle and allow tea to steep about 1 hour.

Remove tea bags, pour tea into 2-quart pitcher. Add 1 cup sugar to warm tea and stir well to dissolve. Fill kettle with water again and add to tea.

Serve warm over ice, or chill. We also serve tea-lemonade—half tea and half lemonade.

PECAN PIE

3 eggs
1 cup light corn syrup
1 cup sugar
1 teaspoon vanilla
Pinch salt
3 tablespoons melted butter
1¹/₂ cups broken pecans
Unbaked 9-inch pie shell

Combine eggs and syrup thoroughly. Add other ingredients in order. Stir well. Pour in unbaked pie shell. Bake at 350° for 45 to 50 minutes, until sides are set and middle is only slightly jiggly. Pie will rise, then deflate during cooling.

Serves 8.

An Elegant Evening

If Savannah loves the down-and-dirty oyster roast, she also embraces on occasion an evening of elegance, reminiscent of the great parties written about in diaries of the city's earlier prosperous citizens.

Clever debutante parties, opulent weddings and dazzling fundraising galas give Savannahians the chance to dress up and remember their manners. Perhaps the largest, most elaborate, party of the year is the annual Telfair Ball, a themed event revived in 1980 as a fundraiser for the Telfair Museum of Art. Patrons don their finest and come to the equally dressed-up museum for a night of dancing, auction bidding and fine dining.

This meal, created by chef Walter Dasher in the kitchens of 45 South, is special enough to serve before the ball, or for any occasion when you want to bring out the best.

Burgundy Butter

6 cups burgundy wine
2 tablespoons honey
2 sticks unsalted butter,
  room temperature

In large saucepan, reduce wine over high heat, watching so that it does not boil over, until there are only about 4 tablespoons left in the pot. Add honey. Add butter slowly in small pieces, swirling the pot after each addition to combine. Keep warm.

Crispy Scallops and Leeks with Burgundy Butter

2 cups flour seasoned with salt,
  white pepper and cayenne
  pepper
16 large sea scallops, halved
Vegetable oil of your choice for
  frying
Egg wash:
  1 egg
  ¾ cup heavy cream
  2 cups washed, dried and
    julienned leeks
Radicchio leaves
Chopped chives

To make egg wash, combine egg and cream well with fork or wire whisk. Dip scallops into flour mixture, then into egg wash, then back into flour mixture. Shake off excess flour. Fry scallops in deep fryer, or in deep skillet in very hot oil. Fry in small batches

Menu

•

Crispy Scallops And Leeks
With Burgundy Butter

Caesar Salad with
Pesto Croutons

Grilled Veal Chops

French Green Beans

Horseradish Mashed Potatoes

Sherried Wild Mushrooms

Cinnamon Almond Shortbread
Cookies with Fresh Seasonal
Fruits and Raspberry
and Mango Coulis

Crispy Scallops and Leek with Burgundy Butter

until golden and crispy, about 3-5 minutes, depending on size. Drain on paper towels and keep warm.

For leeks, wash carefully, cleaning between layers. Rinse well. Slice into julienned strips. Plunge leeks into very hot oil in deep fry pan with removable fry basket for about 30 seconds, until leeks are golden brown. Be careful; oil splatters when leeks first go in, and leeks will burn quickly.

To assemble the dish: Spoon burgundy butter in center of plate in thin pool to cover. Place a nice radicchio leaf in the center of plate to act as a cup. Place four scallops in the cup and cover with crispy leeks. Sprinkle with chopped chives.

Serves 8.

BASIL PESTO

4 cloves garlic, minced
2 cups fresh basil leaves, rinsed and dried
1/3 cup extra virgin olive oil
1/2 teaspoon salt
1/2 teaspoon freshly ground black pepper

Place garlic and basil in bowl of a food processor. With motor running, slowly drizzle in the oil through the feed tube and process until the basil is pureed. Transfer pesto to bowl and stir in salt and pepper. Refrigerate, covered, until ready to use.

Makes 3/4 cup. Freezes well.

PESTO CROUTONS

Use four slices day-old bread of your choice. Brush with pesto mixture on both sides. Cut into 1/2-inch cubes. Bake at 350° until golden brown, about 4 minutes. Stir and turn at least once. Cool.

Can be frozen. Remove frozen croutons and place in 200-degree oven to recrisp. Cool before adding to salad or soup.

CAESAR SALAD

2 heads Romaine lettuce

Dressing:
   1 tablespoon liquid pasteurized egg product
   2 tablespoons red wine vinegar
   1 tablespoon Worcestershire sauce
   1 tablespoon chopped garlic

1 tablespoon anchovy paste
1/8 teaspoon salt
Pinch white pepper
1 1/2 cups olive oil

2 ounces best quality imported Parmesan cheese

Place first seven dressing ingredients into bowl of a food processor. With motor running, slowly drizzle in oil through feed tube and process until thickened.

Wash and spin dry lettuce. Break small leaves into crosswise halves or thirds. Remove large central ribs. Place Romaine in salad bowl and cover with slightly dampened paper towels.

To prepare salad: Toss lettuce with freshly grated Parmesan cheese and about 1/2 cup dressing, or enough to moisten leaves. Add croutons.

Serves 8.

Note: Pasteurized egg product replaces raw egg to reduce risk of salmonella.

GRILLED VEAL CHOPS

8 10-ounce veal chops, cut 1 1/2 inches thick

Marinade:
  1 cup red wine vinegar
  1 cup balsamic vinegar
  2 tablespoons sugar
  2 tablespoons ketchup
  1 tablespoon Dijon mustard
  2 teaspoons black pepper
  2 crushed garlic cloves
  1 teaspoon cayenne pepper
  1/4 cup olive oil

Combine marinade ingredients with wire whisk. Marinate the chops in glass dish or plastic sealable bags for 1 hour, turning once. Grill chops over hot coals until desired doneness, about 8 minutes per side for medium rare.

Serves 8.

FRENCH GREEN BEANS

1 1/2 to 2 pounds small green beans
1/2 cup chopped shallots
2 tablespoons butter
1/2 cup diced red pepper
Salt, optional

Blanch green beans in boiling salted water for 3 to 5 minutes, then drain. Sauté shallots and red pepper in butter for 3 minutes. Add beans and toss. Salt if desired.

Serves 8.

HORSERADISH MASHED POTATOES

6 Idaho potatoes, peeled and cubed
6 tablespoons unsalted butter at room temperature
3/4 cup heavy cream, heated
2 tablespoons grated horseradish
Salt and white pepper to taste

Place the potatoes in a saucepan, cover with cold water and bring to a boil. Reduce the heat and cook until tender, about 20 to 30 minutes. Drain well. Mash with masher or ricer, adding butter, hot cream, salt and pepper to hot potatoes. Mix until smooth. Add horseradish and serve immediately.
    Serves 8.

SHERRIED WILD MUSHROOMS

1/2 cup shiitake mushrooms
1/2 cup tree oyster mushrooms
1/2 cup chanterelle mushrooms
1/2 cup button mushrooms
4 tablespoons butter
1 cup beef broth
1/2 cup sherry

Slice mushrooms into thin slices and sauté in butter until tender, about 5 minutes. Add sherry and broth and reduce to about 3/4 cup of liquid. Use as a sauce for veal chops.

CINNAMON ALMOND SHORTBREAD COOKIES WITH FRESH SEASONAL FRUITS AND RASPBERRY AND MANGO COULIS

1 stick chilled butter, cut into pieces
3/4 cup sugar
1 egg yolk
2 cups all-purpose flour
Cinnamon sugar, for sprinkling
3/4 cup sliced almonds

In bowl of an electric mixer, cream butter and sugar until light and fluffy. Add egg yolk and mix 30 seconds. Scrape down sides of bowl. Slowly add flour on low speed, stopping after the dough is smooth. Divide dough in half and cover with plastic wrap and refrigerate several hours, or overnight.
    Roll cold dough into 1/8 to 1/4-inch thick circle on floured board or cold marble slab. Cut with large round cookie cutter. Place on non-stick cookie sheet. Sprinkle with cinnamon sugar. Press a half dozen or so almonds onto each cookie. Bake cookies in preheated 350° oven on center rack for 9 to 11 minutes.
    Makes 16 cookies. Cookies freeze well.

RASPBERRY AND MANGO COULIS

2 cups fresh or frozen raspberries
1/2 cup confectioners' sugar
1 tablespoon fresh lemon juice

Purée raspberries in blender or food processor. Add sugar and lemon juice. Process until smooth. Strain sauce to remove seeds.

1 large mango, fresh and ripe
¹/4 cup sugar
1 tablespoon fresh lemon juice

Slit the skin on the mango the whole way around and peel off skin. With spoon remove all flesh that remains on skin. Slice flesh off the pit. Purée mango flesh with the sugar and lemon juice in blender or food processor. Strain sauce to remove any bits of mango fiber.

2 cups heavy cream
¹/2 vanilla bean
¹/4 cup granulated sugar

Grate vanilla bean into sugar. In chilled mixing bowl, whip cream with chilled beaters at medium speed until cream forms soft peaks. Add sugar slowly until cream is light, thick and stiff. Avoid overbeating.

To assemble: Place one cookie on each plate, almond-side up. Cover with ¹/2 cup of whipped cream. Top with fresh fruit of your choice (whole raspberries, sliced strawberries or finely diced peaches are beautiful). Put another cookie on top, almond side up. Use the two different sauces to accent the base of the cookies. Garnish with mint sprigs.

Best of Bailee's Jewish Cooking

Five months after James Edward Oglethorpe colonized Georgia, 42 Jews arrived—35 from Portugal and the rest from Germany. The congregation called themselves Mickve Israel—the Hope of Israel. Although the congregation was chartered by Gov. Edward Telfair in 1790, it was almost 100 years—on April 11, 1878—before the consecration of their third synagogue on Monterey Square, where the current congregation worships. Built in English Gothic style, Temple Mickve Israel attracts thousands of tourists each year. Mickve Israel is recognized as the third oldest Jewish congregation in America and the oldest in the South. Savannah's Jewish families, numbering a mere 3,000, have throughout the city's history been at the forefront of the city's business, cultural, political and social activity, and have evolved into three congregations—Temple Mickve Israel, Agudath Achim and B'nai B'rith Jacob.

Talented cook and artist Bailee Kronowitz, a member of congregation Agudath Achim, created this menu after being issued the challenge: "If your children were to return for the weekend and request their favorite dishes,

what would they be?" The results of her efforts were served to special friends on treasured heirlooms in the art-filled townhouse Bailee shares with her husband Ronald in Savannah's historic district.

CHOPPED CHICKEN LIVER

1 pound chicken livers
3 large hard-boiled eggs,
  boiled gently for 12
  minutes and allowed to
  cool for 20 minutes before
  peeling
2 large onions, finely chopped
2 tablespoons (or more)
  chicken fat (schmaltz*)
Salt and pepper, freshly
  ground to taste

Sauté three-fourths of the onions in chicken fat until golden. Add livers and sauté until cooked through and no pink shows.

Place livers, sautéed onions, boiled eggs, raw onions and salt and pepper in food mill or ricer and grind until smooth. Or, chop in food processor until you have

---

MENU
•
CHOPPED CHICKEN LIVER

BEEF BRISKET

WHOLE STUFFED BAKED FISH

POTATO LATKES

VEGETABLE MOUSSE

BRIOCHE OR CHALLAH

GEORGIA PECAN CLUSTERS

CHOCOLATE MOUSSE

spreading consistency; do not purée. Add a little more chicken fat if too dry. Adjust seasonings.

Refrigerate in crock or mold until serving time. Serve with bland crackers on lettuce-lined plate.

*To make schmaltz: Sauté chicken fat and skin in pan until fat is rendered. Remove all but the liquid fat. Add a little onion to fat for flavor if desired. Drain out onions. Freeze schmaltz in small portions and use as necessary.

Serves 10 to 12 as part of a large meal.

Beef Brisket

1 beef brisket, about 8 to 10 pounds
Juice of 1 or 2 lemons
2 cans tomato soup
1/3 cup brown sugar
2 cups ketchup
5 large onions, sliced
Salt and freshly ground pepper to taste

In heavy frying pan, sear brisket on both sides. Line large roasting pan with heavy-duty foil. Combine onions, soup, ketchup, brown sugar and lemon juice. Place half of mixture on bottom of foil. Top with brisket. Add rest of onion mixture on top of brisket. Cover with foil and crimp tightly. Bake at 275° overnight, or 8 hours. Refrigerate 8 hours. Remove all fat from meat and any that congeals on top of sauce. Slice meat thinly on the bias. Place slices in foil-lined pan, completely covering with sauce. Add water if sauce is too thick. Cook overnight again at 275°. Refrigerate again. Skim fat. Before serving, reheat at 325° at least an hour or more.

Serves 10 to 12 as part of large meal.

Whole Stuffed Baked Fish

1 whole trout or bass, any variety, about 5 pounds
1 medium onion, sliced on diagonal
2 large carrots, sliced on diagonal
2 large celery ribs, sliced on diagonal
3 cloves garlic, crushed

For dry rub:
 1/4 teaspoon salt
 3 to 4 grinds of fresh pepper
 1/2 teaspoon dried thyme
 1/2 teaspoon dried tarragon
 1/2 teaspoon dried basil
 1/4 teaspoon garlic powder
 1/2 teaspoon lemon and herb spice

For basting:
 3 tablespoons lemon juice
 2 1/2 tablespoons Worcestershire sauce
 3 to 4 tablespoons butter

Have fish market gut and scale fish, leaving head and tail intact. You may also wish to have fish butterflied, which removes interior bones, but leaves head and tail, and makes for easier serving of fish portions. Wash fish to remove loose scales. Slit underside of fish to the bone. Clean well.

Make mix of the herbs and spices. Rub inside and outside of fish.

Fill cavity of fish with combined vegetables and garlic. Close cavity by basting sides together with trussing needle and white cotton string, or by skewering sides together. Place any remaining vegetables in bottom of roasting pan. Place fish on top.

Combine lemon juice and Worcestershire sauce. Pour on top of fish. Dot with butter. Bake in a 375° oven for about 30 to 40 minutes. Test for doneness by twisting a fork on the underside; fish should appear cooked through but should not flake. Place on pretty fish platter. Serve surrounded by lemon slices and extra vegetables.

Serves 6 to 8 as part of a large meal.

POTATO LATKES

2 to 3 medium baking potatoes
1 to 2 medium yellow onions
Salt and pepper to taste
1 egg, well-beaten
1 to 2 tablespoons flour
Vegetable oil for frying

Peel and wash potatoes. Cut into medium chunks and place in cold water. Peel onions and cut into quarters. Dry potato chunks and drop one into blender. Process at medium to high speed until finely chopped. Continue adding potatoes, processing after each one.

Process onion separately. Combine chopped potato and onion and well-beaten egg in blender, or by hand. Mix well. Add 1 to 2 tablespoons flour until mixture is slightly thick. Drop by large tablespoons into sizzling hot oil. Cook on one side until brown, about 3 to 5 minutes. Turn and cook on other side until brown. Drain on paper towels.

Serve hot with applesauce and sour cream.

Pancakes can be made in advance and refrigerated. When ready to serve, place pancakes in single layer on cookie sheet and heat for about 5 minutes at 350°.

Makes about 30 small pancakes.

VEGETABLE MOUSSE

2 pounds broccoli florets
2 pounds cauliflower florets
2 pounds carrots, washed, peeled and sliced
  into 1/2-inch pieces
Salt to taste
1/2 cup milk (optional)
8 tablespoons butter
1 1/2 teaspoons freshly grated nutmeg
Freshly ground pepper to taste

Prepare vegetables, breaking or cutting into uniform-size pieces. Keep a few broccoli florets and parboil them for about two minutes, then cool under running water to set color, for garnish, if desired. Cook remaining broccoli, cauliflower and carrots separately in a heavy-bottomed saucepan with about 2 inches of salted water. Cook until tender, about 12 minutes for carrots and broccoli and about 15 to 18 minutes for cauliflower. You may add milk to cauliflower water to keep it white, if desired.

When each vegetable is fork-tender, drain and immediately place in cold water to set color. Drain immediately.

Purée each cooked vegetable in blender or food processor with two tablespoons butter, 1/2 teaspoon nutmeg and salt and pepper to taste.

Butter a shallow, attractive glass dish and layer broccoli mousse, carrot mousse and cauliflower mousse. Decorate with broccoli florets, if desired. Or, save a little carrot mousse and pipe this on top of cauliflower mousse in decorative pattern. Dot with remaining 2 tablespoons butter.

Bake at 400° until vegetables are heated through and butter is melted, about 20 minutes.

Serves 10 to 12 as part of large meal.

Note: Jewish cooks who keep kosher cannot cook cauliflower with milk if this dish is to be served with meat or poultry. The milk helps to keep the cauliflower white and gives it the appearance of mashed potatoes. If you are serving this dish with meat or poultry, substitute Mazola green package margarine or other nondairy or pareve margarine for butter.

BRIOCHE OR CHALLAH

1 tablespoon yeast
1/4 cup warm water (105°-115°)
1/2 cup softened butter or margarine
1/3 cup sugar
1/2 teaspoon salt
1/2 cup milk
3 1/4 cups flour, all-purpose
3 beaten eggs
1 beaten yolk (reserve white)
1 tablespoon sugar

Soften yeast in warm water. Heat milk to 105°-115°. Thoroughly cream butter, sugar and salt. Add milk and 1 cup flour. Mix well. Add yeast, 3 beaten eggs and extra yolk, beating well before adding remaining flour. Beat 5 to 8 minutes longer. Put dough in clean bowl and cover with dry towel; let double in bulk (about 2 hours). Stir down, beating well. Cover with plastic wrap and refrigerate overnight.

Brioche: Stir down dough. Turn out on lightly floured surface. Divide dough in fourths, setting aside one-fourth. Cut three remaining pieces in half and shape each piece into 4 balls, making 24 in all. Tuck under cut edges, placing each in well-greased muffin tins or brioche containers. With finger, make an indentation in top of each ball and place a small ball, shaped from the remaining fourth, on top of each roll. Let rise, covered with dry towel, until doubled, about 1 hour. Combine slightly beaten egg white with 1 tablespoon sugar; brush tops. Bake at 350° to 375° for 15 minutes, or until well-browned and hollow when tapped. Take bread out of pans and place on wire racks. Serve warm.

Challah: Stir down. Turn out on slightly floured

surface. Divide dough into 6 pieces and roll each into a long piece, after dusting with flour. Braid 3 pieces together and place on greased baking sheet. Braid 3 pieces together and place on top of first braid. Cover and let rise until double. Brush top with egg white and sugar mixture and bake at 350° for 25 to 35 minutes, or until done. Let cool on wire rack.

When bread comes from oven, rub top of brioche or challah with cold stick of butter or margarine to make a glorious finish.

Note: This bread cannot be used for Passover, a Jewish holiday when Matzoh is substituted for bread. In order to use this bread at a meal when meat is served, substitute Coffee Rich for milk and Mazola green package or other non-dairy margarine for butter or margarine.

GEORGIA PECAN CLUSTERS

1 egg white, beaten stiffly
1 cup dark or light-brown sugar
2 cups pecans, coarsely chopped or broken into large
*   pieces*

Preheat oven to 450°. Beat egg white until stiff. Add brown sugar and beat for 30 seconds, until blended. Mix in nuts with spoon, saving 2 to 3 tablespoons to add at the end when batter is low on nuts. Drop by teaspoonfuls on greased cookie sheets at least 1 inch apart.

Turn off oven and place pans in oven. Let stand at least 1 hour before opening oven. Let cool and crisp on rack. Store in air-tight container.

Makes 18 to 24.

CHOCOLATE MOUSSE

4 squares (4 ounces) unsweetened chocolate
¾ cup sugar
¼ cup water
5 egg yolks
1 cup whipping cream, whipped
1 teaspoon vanilla extract or Kahlua® or Frangelico®

Combine chocolate, sugar and water in top of a double boiler. Heat until the chocolate has melted, stirring occasionally. Add egg yolks, one at a time, while the double boiler is still over the heat, beating hard with whisk after each addition. Remove mixture from stove and off hot water, but continue to beat for a minute while mixture cools. Whip cream, adding flavoring. Fold into cooled chocolate mixture. Turn into dessert bowl or individual sherbet glasses and let stand in the refrigerator at least 12 hours.

Makes 8 servings.

THE OYSTER ROAST

Before English settlers arrived in Savannah, the area was inhabited by Indians, who located their villages close to tidal creeks, providing them with plenty of seafood to eat. According to research conducted in 1970 by Lewis Larson Jr. of West Georgia College in Carrollton concerning the aboriginal diet along the Southeastern coast, these Native Americans were primarily gatherers, and did little farming. They ate much of their food raw, but they did toss oysters into the fire to force them to pop open, a wonderful idea that has endured along the coast in the form of the winter oyster roast.

Savannahians prefer to have oyster roasts in the coldest weather, when oysters are plump. This is a dress down kind of party, a time to pull out your college jeans and your favorite raggedy sweater. It is both proper and resourceful to arrive with an oyster knife stuck in your jeans' pocket, and to bring a cotton glove. The knife is for popping the oysters open once the fire has loosened the hinges a bit, and the glove protects the hand from the steaming oysters' sharp edges or a slipping knife blade.

Oyster lovers who plan roasts don't typically coddle their guests. They often serve little else but oysters. But chili, Brunswick stew and other hearty concoctions do offer warmth and a little filler for those who never quite developed a taste for oysters.

HOW TO ROAST OYSTERS

1 bushel of oysters per 6 to 10 people

Pick through oysters, discarding any open ones. Hose off oysters thoroughly. They may open up if they take in too much water; if so, tap to close.

To roast, shovel cleaned oysters in single layer on thick piece of preheated metal placed over hot wood fire or into a steamer. Cover oysters with water-soaked burlap sacks. Steam oysters until they pop open. The more you steam, the more shriveled and less juicy the oysters will be.

When open, shovel oysters from metal to table. Add more raw oysters to the fire. Release oyster from shell with oyster knife. Eat oysters with cocktail

---

MENU

•

BEER

OYSTERS

COCKTAIL SAUCE

MELTED BUTTER

SALTINES

CHILI OR BRUNSWICK STEW

SAVANNAH PRALINES

---

sauce and melted butter and plenty of fresh saltines.

Roasted or steamed oysters that aren't eaten can be shucked and refrigerated to be used in oyster stew.

Anyone can throw an impromptu oyster roast. Lay oysters in a single layer in a disposable roaster. Cover with wet tea towel. Place on gas grill. Lower lid. Steam until oysters pop. They also can be steamed in your oven.

COCKTAIL SAUCE

2 cups ketchup
2 teaspoons horseradish (or more, to taste)
Juice of 1 lemon or 1 lime

Combine. Chill. Serve with seafood.

CHILI

3 tablespoons butter or margarine
1 large onion, chopped
1 green pepper, chopped
2 cloves garlic, pressed or minced
1 pound ground beef
1 16-ounce can chopped tomatoes
1 16-ounce can filled with water
1 teaspoon celery seed
1/2 teaspoon cayenne pepper
2 tablespoons chili powder
1 teaspoon dried basil
1/2 teaspoon salt
1 16-ounce can kidney beans (optional),
  light or dark, undrained

In large Dutch oven, sauté onion, green pepper and garlic in butter for about a minute. Add ground beef and brown. Drain off fat.

Add all other ingredients except kidney beans and bring to a boil. Reduce heat and allow to simmer about 2 hours, uncovered, until sauce is thick. Add beans about 10 minutes before serving.

Serves 6 to 8. Freezes well.

BRUNSWICK STEW

2 chickens
1 large pork roast
3 quarts water
Salt, to taste
Freshly grated black pepper, to taste
1/2 teaspoon cayenne pepper
3 medium onions, chopped
2 cups corn kernels, fresh, if possible
2 cups lima beans
4 potatoes, any variety, diced
2 16-ounce cans tomatoes, chopped
1 15-ounce can small garden peas
1/2 cup vinegar
1 stick butter
Tomato paste

Cook chickens and pork roast in water with salt and pepper until tender. Cool. Remove meat from bones and return meat to stock. Add onions, corn, lima beans, potatoes, tomatoes, peas and vinegar. Simmer, with lid off, for several hours, stirring frequently to keep from scorching. Before serving, add butter and color with tomato paste, if necessary. Taste and adjust seasonings, adding salt and pepper if needed.

Serves 10 to 12. Freezes well.

SAVANNAH PRALINES

3 tablespoons butter
1½ cups light brown sugar
½ cup whipping cream
1 tablespoon corn syrup
1 cup pecans
1 cup vanilla extract

Melt butter in heavy saucepan. Stir in brown sugar, whipping cream and corn syrup. Bring to a boil, then lower heat to medium-low. Slow bubbles should continue. Cook 10 minutes, stirring constantly, making sure not to let mixture burn. Add pecans. Stir and cook 5 minutes more at same temperature. (Temperature will reach about 200° on candy thermometer.) Remove pan from heat. Add vanilla to mixture. Stir vigorously to blend. Drop mixture by tablespoonfuls onto waxed paper sprayed with vegetable spray. Allow to cool, then store immediately in tins.

Makes 8 pralines.

Spreading the Oysters

A Formal Fish Dinner

In the 1950s, Savannah, like other cities, was intent on tearing down that which was old. But in 1954, a handful of civic-minded ladies, distressed over the leveling of the old City Market on Ellis Square, got together and raised enough money to buy the Davenport House, built in 1820. The group became Historic Savannah Foundation Inc., a non-profit agency dedicated to the preservation of the old and a proper blending of the new. The Davenport House was restored in 1962, and remains open for visitation.

The Savannah Historic District is one of the nation's largest urban landmark districts. It includes more than 2,300 architecturally and historically significant buildings in a 2.5 square-mile area. Each year, historic inns and private homes are open for touring, and visitors are enthralled by the high ceilings, architectural designs and decorative arts—antiques, handmade rugs and other collectibles.

This elegant, leisurely meal begins with martinis and a colorful cheese spread, proceeds to oysters broiled to perfection, features fresh fish of your choice and concludes with a smooth crème caramel.

The menu is regally presented on the owner's collection of silver and china set against a stunning backdrop of fine English antiques. What a way to while away a winter evening!

The Perfect Martini

Per drink:
2 ounces Bombay
Sapphire gin
Splash dry vermouth
1 black olive

Place black olive in glass. Shake gin and vermouth over ice. Pour beverage over black olive.

Pesto and Tomato Terrine

2 sticks softened butter
8 ounces softened cream cheese
1/2 cup pesto
1/2 cup sun-dried tomato pesto

Mix butter and cream cheese with mixer until well-combined. Cut off top of half-gal-

---

Menu
•
The Perfect Martini

Pesto and Tomato Terrine
with Crackers

Oysters with Green Sauce

Carrot Ginger Soup

Pan-Fried Flounder
OR
Pecan-Coated Grouper
OR
Shad with Roe

Oven-Roasted Garlic Potatoes

Asparagus with Lemon Butter

Kacey's Cheese Biscuits

Individual Crème Caramels
with Benne Wafers

Madeira of your Choice

---

lon paper milk carton, leaving about 4 inches depth. Line with waxed paper, leaving enough to fold over top. Alternate layers of cheese mixture and fillings, starting and ending with cream-cheese mixture. Cover and refrigerate at least 2 hours. Peel away carton. Garnish with fresh basil leaves. Can be prepared several days in advance. Serve with bland crackers.

Serves 8 to 10.

PESTO

1½ cups firmly packed fresh basil leaves
⅓ cup grated Parmesan cheese
2 cloves garlic, peeled
¼ cup pine nuts or pecans
½ teaspoon salt
⅓ cup olive oil

Place everything but oil in food processor. Process until well-blended. Add olive oil slowly.

Makes about 1 cup. Freezes well.

SUN-DRIED TOMATO PESTO

½ cup drained sun-dried tomatoes
¼ cup olive oil from tomatoes
1½ teaspoons cayenne pepper (optional)

Blend well in food processor.

OYSTERS WITH GREEN SAUCE

32 oysters on the half shell

4 slices bacon
¼ cup butter or margarine, melted
⅓ cup parsley, chopped
1 tablespoon lemon juice
⅓ cup soft bread crumbs
Rock salt

Place oyster halves in shallow baking pan that has been lined with rock salt.

Cook bacon until crisp. Drain; reserve drippings. Combine crumbled bacon, bacon drippings, butter or margarine, parsley and lemon juice. Top each oyster with approximately 1 teaspoon of the mixture. Sprinkle on bread crumbs. May be covered and refrigerated at this point.

Bake at 450° for 10 to 12 minutes.

Serve with green sauce.

Serves 8.

GREEN SAUCE

1 cup chopped parsley
¼ cup chopped green onion
2 tablespoons capers
1 clove minced garlic
⅔ cup mayonnaise
2 tablespoons olive oil
1 tablespoon lemon juice
½ teaspoon prepared mustard

Combine parsley, green onion, capers and garlic in blender or food processor. Add mayonnaise, olive oil, lemon juice and mustard. Blend. Chill. Serve with oysters.

Carrot Ginger Soup

¹/₄ cup butter
¹/₂ cup chopped green onion
3 cups peeled sliced carrots
1 teaspoon sugar
1 teaspoon fresh ginger, finely minced
¹/₄ teaspoon cinnamon
1 tablespoon flour
Salt and pepper to taste
1¹/₂ cups chicken broth
1¹/₂ cups water
2 cups freshly squeezed orange juice
³/₄ cup heavy cream

Melt butter. Sauté onions until tender, about 2 minutes. Stir in carrots, sugar, ginger and cinnamon. Cook 3 minutes. Add flour, salt and pepper and toss to coat carrots. Cook 1 minute. Add chicken broth, water and orange juice. Bring to a boil, reduce heat to low, cover and simmer about 20 minutes, until carrots are tender.

In blender, purée until smooth. Pour into a bowl, add cream and blend well. Chill.

Garnish with orange slices, fresh parsley or dill.

Makes 8 ³/₄-cup servings. If soup bowls are large, make 1¹/₂ times the recipe.

Pan-Fried Flounder

4 skinless flounder fillets
Salt and pepper to taste
Flour for dredging fish
2 tablespoons vegetable oil
3 tablespoons butter, divided

Juice of 1 lemon
1 bottle capers

Wash fillets in cold water and pat dry. Salt and pepper. Dredge fillets in flour. Place oil and 2 tablespoons butter in flat, heavy-bottomed skillet and heat on medium-high until butter melts. Keeping heat at medium-high, cook fish on one side about 3 minutes (more or less, depending on size of fillets), until deep brown and crispy. Turn fish and cook on second side, about 3 minutes. TURN FISH ONLY ONCE.

Remove fish to serving platter.

Turn off heat. Into hot skillet, whisk in remaining 1 tablespoon butter. Add lemon juice. Pour in capers, liquid and all. Whisk. Pour thin sauce over fish fillets.

Serve at once.

Serves 4. If serving 8, cook 4 other fillets in a separate pan exactly in this manner. Or, serve half-portions of flounder and half portions of grouper or shad.

PECAN-COATED GROUPER

4 grouper fillets
About 1/2 cup melted butter for coating fillets
1 tablespoon butter, for cooking fish
1 tablespoon oil
1 cup pecans, minced into crumbs
  in food processor

Roll fillets in melted butter. Coat with pecans, pressing nuts into fish. In cast-iron or other heavy, ovenproof skillet, heat 1 tablespoon butter and 1 tablespoon oil. When sizzling, sear fish on both sides in skillet, about 2 minutes per side. Place fish in skillet in oven at 350° for 6 to 10 minutes, depending on thickness of fish.

Serve immediately.

Serves 4. For 8 guests, prepare eight fillets in two skillets, or serve half portions of grouper with half portions of flounder or shad.

SHAD WITH ROE

1 boned shad
2 pairs shad roe
Juice from one lemon
1 teaspoon seasoned salt, divided
1/2 teaspoon paprika
2 tablespoons butter
4-6 slices bacon

Drizzle lemon juice over shad and sprinkle with half of seasoned salt and paprika. Dot with butter. Sprinkle roe with rest of seasoned salt. Wrap roe with bacon, completely encasing roe. Secure bacon with toothpicks.

Place shad and roe in greased baking pan and bake in preheated 400-degree oven for 10 minutes. Baste with pan juices. Turn heat to broil and brown fish, about 3 minutes. Remove fish from pan and continue broiling roe until bacon is crisp, turning if needed. Or, cook roe separately in a frying pan.

Serves 4 to 6. If serving 8, buy larger shad fillets. Or, serve half portions of shad with flounder or grouper.

OVEN-ROASTED GARLIC POTATOES

16 large new potatoes, washed
  and cubed into relatively uniform chunks
1 tablespoon olive oil
1 clove garlic, finely minced
Salt to taste

Season olive oil with salt and minced garlic. Place mixture and potatoes in large plastic bag. Toss to coat. Roast potatoes at 350° in glass baking dish sprayed with vegetable spray for about 30 to 40 minutes, until crisp on the outside, tender inside.

ASPARAGUS WITH LEMON BUTTER

2 pounds fresh asparagus/thin stalks preferred
4 tablespoons butter
Juice of 1 lemon

Wash asparagus. Line asparagus up on a cutting board with the tops even. Even up bottoms, cutting as little stalk as possible. If stalks are thin and tender, it is not necessary to peel them. If stalks are large, peel them with a vegetable peeler.

Bring a skillet or oval casserole filled half full of

salted water to boil. Dump in asparagus all at once. When water returns to the boil, cook asparagus from 1 to 5 minutes, depending on its size and your preference.

Immediately drain and serve hot. Or, prepare in advance, refrigerate in clean, damp towels and reheat by dumping briefly into boiling water. Can also be served cold, with vinaigrette, but not with butter sauce.

To make sauce: Melt butter. Whisk in lemon juice. Pour over asparagus, or serve sauce separately.

KACEY'S CHEESE BISCUITS

3/4 cup butter, room temperature
1 1/2 cups grated sharp Cheddar cheese
1/4 cup Parmesan cheese
1/2 teaspoon salt
1 1/2 cups all-purpose flour

In food processor, cream butter and cheeses. Sift together salt and flour. Add to butter-cheese mixture. Pulse processor. Blend just until mixture forms a ball. Mixture will be soft. Spoon out evenly onto two pieces of waxed paper and wrap paper around cheese, forming with hands into a long roll about the diameter of a silver dollar. Refrigerate until firm. Slice into 1/2-inch thick slices on unbuttered non-stick cookie sheets. Bake at 350° for 12 to 15 minutes.

Makes about 40 biscuits. Dough freezes well.

INDIVIDUAL CRÈME CARAMELS

For caramel:
1 cup sugar
3 tablespoons water

For the custard:
6 large eggs
5 egg yolks
3/4 cup sugar
3 cups milk
1 cup heavy cream
2 or more teaspoons vanilla extract

To prepare caramel, heat sugar and water in heavy saucepan until sugar is dissolved. Cover the pan and cook over medium heat until bubbles are large and thick. Uncover. Keep cooking over medium heat, stirring constantly, until liquid turns to a light brown. Pour quickly into large custard dish or individual custard dishes, enough syrup to coat bottom of dish or dishes.

For custard, beat eggs, egg yolks and sugar until light yellow. Heat milk and cream until hot but not boiling. Add milk to egg mixture, beating constantly. Add vanilla. Strain mixture into mold or molds lined with caramelized sugar. Place mold or molds into a pan of hot water 1 inch deep.

Bake at 325° for 45 minutes or so for large mold, 20 to 25 minutes for individual ones. Custard is done when knife inserted an inch from sides comes out clean. Center will still be slightly undercooked.

Cool, then chill, covered with plastic wrap.

To unmold, dip mold or molds into hot water to the depth of the caramel. Hold in hot water about 10 seconds. Unmold custard on serving dish. Caramel will melt and slide down sides. Serve immediately.

Makes 8 small cream caramels, or one 8-by-8-inch caramel.

Serve with benne wafers. (Recipe in a Gullah Board Meeting Buffet, page 84).

IN THE SPIRIT OF ST. PATRICK'S DAY

By the 1860s, Irish and other Europeans made up half of Savannah's population. The early Irish were community-minded and gregarious by nature, always fond of visiting and talking.

That community-minded, gregarious Irish spirit continues in Savannah on St. Patrick's Day, when everyone becomes Irish for the day. Ceremonies are both religious and outlandish, solemn and celebratory, and culminate with the St. Patrick's Day Parade, which attracts an estimated 300,000 viewers.

This menu celebrates the spirit of the day with a hearty stew—a nostalgic recipe prepared by our host and hostesses each year around St. Patrick's Day in observance of their anniversary. A tart salad and rosemary soda muffins are all that are needed to complete the meal. Champagne Midoris, an ice cream parfait flavored with crème de menthe, and Irish coffee help to keep guests in a festive mood.

CHAMPAGNE MIDORIS

Fill champagne glasses with champagne. Add 1 teaspoon Midori® liqueur.

MENU

•

CHAMPAGNE MIDORIS

PARTY REUBENS

SPINACH AND APPLE SALAD

MR. ROBERT'S IRISH STEW
WITH SHAMROCK TOAST

IRISH SODA MUFFINS WITH
WHITE CHEDDAR AND ROSEMARY

WHIPPED LEPRECHAUNS

IRISH COFFEE

PARTY REUBENS

48 slices party rye bread
2 pounds medium to thinly sliced deli corned beef,
* cut to fit bread*
2 cups sauerkraut, drained
Sliced Swiss cheese (If using presliced cheese, one slice
* will make 4 party sandwiches)*
½ cup mayonnaise
2 tablespoons chili sauce
1 tablespoon horseradish
2 teaspoons Dijon mustard
Melted butter, about ¼ cup

Combine mayonnaise, chili sauce, horseradish and mustard. Set aside. Spread sauce lightly on both sides of bread with pastry brush. Layer corned beef, Swiss cheese and teaspoon of sauerkraut. Place sandwiches on cookie sheet. Lightly brush bread with melted butter; broil until barely browned. To prevent edges from curling, cover with foil and place another cookie sheet on top with weights. Just before serving, turn sandwiches, lightly brush with melted butter and broil.
Makes 24 small sandwiches.

SPINACH AND APPLE SALAD

4 bunches fresh spinach, washed, dried
* and stems removed*
1 cup red onion rings, thinly sliced
1 cup pecans, coarsely chopped
1 Granny Smith apple, cored and thinly sliced

Dressing:
* 3 tablespoons lemon juice*
* 1/2 cup vegetable oil*
* 2 tablespoons sugar*
* 1 small clove garlic, crushed*
* 1 teaspoon salt*

Whisk together dressing ingredients. Place spinach leaves on plates and top with red onion rings, pecans and apple slices. Pour dressing over all.
  Serves 8.

MR. ROBERT'S IRISH STEW WITH SHAMROCK TOAST

3 pounds leg-of-lamb meat, cut into 1 1/2-inch squares,
* bone reserved*
For stock:
* Lamb bone*
* 2 whole onions*
* 2 carrots, cut in large chunks*
* 3 ribs celery, halved*
* 1 bay leaf*
* 1 garlic clove, crushed*
* Salt and pepper*
* 2 quarts water*

For Stew:
* 1/4 cup Canola oil*
* 1/4 cup olive oil*
* 6 celery stalks, chopped, including tops and leaves*
* 2 large Spanish onions, chopped*
* 2 cups chopped leeks*
* 4 cups finely chopped cabbage*
* 1/2 teaspoon ground mace*
* 1/2 teaspoon ground coriander*
* 1/2 teaspoon ground thyme*
* 2 14.5-ounce cans diced tomatoes, drained, juice*
*   reserved*
* 8 large baking potatoes, peeled and chopped*
* Spring garden peas for garnish*

Heavily salt lamb chunks and place in covered glass dish overnight in refrigerator.
  For stock: Combine stock ingredients. Allow to cook, without lid, several hours, until flavor is rich and liquid is reduced to about 1 quart. Remove bone and vegetables. Strain stock for stew.
  For stew: In large oven-proof Dutch oven, sauté lamb chunks in canola oil and set aside. Add 1/4 cup olive oil and sauté celery, onions, chopped leeks and cabbage. Add seasonings, tomatoes and potatoes. Return meat to pot. Add 3 cups stock. (Freeze remaining stock for another use.) Cover and bring stew to a boil, then place in 350-degree oven for 1 1/2 hours, until meat is tender.
  Remove meat from stew and set aside.
  Purée remaining ingredients and return to pot with meat. Bring to boil again. When serving, top with spring garden peas and shamrock toast on the side.
  To make shamrock toast: Use any homemade bread. Slice about 1/4 inch thick. Make cutouts with shamrock cookie cutter. Toast lightly.
  Serves 8 to 10.

Mr. Robert's Irish Stew

IRISH SODA MUFFINS WITH WHITE CHEDDAR AND ROSEMARY

3 cups all-purpose flour
1 cup whole wheat flour
2 teaspoons baking powder
1½ teaspoons salt
1 teaspoon baking soda
¼ cup (½ stick) well-chilled butter, cut into pieces
6 ounces coarsely grated white Cheddar cheese
¼ cup fresh rosemary, snipped finely
  with kitchen shears
2 cups buttermilk
1 egg, beaten to blend

Preheat oven to 350°. Generously grease 2 12-cup muffin tins. Sift together flours, baking powder, salt and baking soda in large bowl. Cut in butter until mixture resembles coarse meal. Stir in cheese and rosemary. Mix buttermilk and egg and add to dry ingredients, stirring just until blended (batter will be thick). Spoon batter into prepared muffin tins. Bake until golden, about 20 minutes. Serve warm.

To freeze, cool thoroughly. Wrap tightly in aluminum foil and place in freezer baggies. To serve, bring to room temperature. Warm in oven for about 15 minutes at 300° just before serving.

WHIPPED LEPRECHAUNS

1 package chocolate wafers, crushed
½ gallon vanilla ice cream
½ cup crème de menthe
½ cup crème de menthe (for garnish)
1 cup heavy cream, whipped
Mint leaves or chocolate mint candy

Thaw ice cream until soft. Mix ½ cup crème de menthe with ice cream. Alternate layers of crushed wafers and ice cream in parfait glasses. Freeze.

Before serving, top with dollop of whipped cream and pour slight amount of crème de menthe over whipped cream. Garnish with mint leaves or chocolate mint candy.

Makes 8 parfaits.

IRISH COFFEE

For each cup:
  Lemon and sugar
  ½ to 1 ounce Irish whiskey
  ½ to ¾ cup hot, strong black coffee
  1-2 teaspoons sugar
  2 tablespoons lightly whipped cream

Rub lemon slice around rim of glass mug. Dip in sugar to coat rim of glass. Pour in coffee. Add sugar and stir. Add whiskey. Slide whipped cream off of spoon so that it floats on top of coffee.

PLANTATION BRUNCH

At the end of a mile-long alley of magnificent live oaks are the tabby remains of Wormsloe, the colonial estate of Noble Jones, who came to Savannah with James Oglethorpe aboard the ship *Anne* in 1733. Jones—a physician and carpenter who served as a soldier, constable, rum agent, surveyor and member of the Royal Council—was one of only a handful of original settlers to survive in the new Georgia colony. Wormsloe's tabby ruins and nature trails are now owned by the state and are open for touring. Nearby is a plantation house, built in 1828, that has always been the private home to Jones' descendants.

Wormsloe Plantation in early spring is a sight to behold, with blooming camellias, some dating back to the Civil War, and footpaths leading visitors serenely past wisteria, magnolia, dogwood, Cherokee rose and other native shrubs, ending at the edge of a fast-moving river.

Such a splendid view deserves a splendid brunch like this one that begins in the elegant main dining room of the plantation house with mimosas or mint juleps, then proceeds to a bountiful buffet of Southern brunch dishes, updated and refined, to be eaten on the screened porch.

MENU

•

MINT JULEPS OR MIMOSAS

COUNTRY HAM BISCUITS

SAUSAGE-STUFFED VIDALIA ONIONS

TOMATO PIE

SHRIMP AND GRITS

CHEESE BLINTZ CASSEROLE

FRESH FRUIT WITH BOILED DRESSING

BREAKFAST YEAST RING

MINT JULEPS

Mint syrup
Kentucky bourbon
Crushed ice
Mint sprigs for garnish

MINT SYRUP

1 cup sugar
1 cup water
2 cups lightly packed fresh
mint

Combine sugar and water in saucepan. Bring to a boil, stirring gently to dissolve, then boil 5 minutes without stirring. Remove from heat, add mint and cover saucepan. Let sit until cool. Strain into jar. Keep refrigerated. Makes about 1½ cups.

For each drink, fill tall glass with crushed ice. Add 1 jigger mint syrup and 1½ jiggers bourbon. Stir. Add more ice if necessary. Garnish with sprig of mint.

MIMOSAS

Champagne
Orange juice
Fresh mint

Fill each champagne or wine glass half full with orange juice, then add champagne. Garnish with fresh mint sprigs.

COUNTRY HAM BISCUITS

(See Christmas Eve Buffet, page 111)

SAUSAGE-STUFFED VIDALIA ONIONS*

6 medium sweet Vidalia onions
6 tablespoons butter
Salt and pepper, to taste

STUFFING

1 pound spicy sausage
2 cups onions, chopped, removed from center of onions
2 ounces white cheddar cheese, grated

BUTTER SAUCE

1 teaspoon olive oil
2 tablespoons vermouth
3 tablespoons orange juice
1 tablespoon chopped Vidalia onion
1 small garlic clove, minced
2 tablespoons heavy cream
1 stick butter, cut in pieces

Peel onions. Scoop out centers with sharp spoon, leaving an onion cup. Chop centers for stuffing and sauce. Place onions in a shallow baking dish and place 1 tablespoon butter in each onion. Bake onions at 350° for 45 minutes, or until very tender. Or, microwave in circular dish for 12 minutes, rotating dish halfway through cooking time.

For stuffing, combine minced onion and sausage in skillet. Sauté until brown. Drain well. Toss sausage with cheese. Spoon stuffing into cavity of each cooked onion.

For butter sauce, simmer olive oil, vermouth, orange juice, onion and garlic in saucepan. Reduce by half. Remove from heat. Add cream, return to heat and add butter bit by bit, whisking after each addition. Keep in thermos until time to serve onions.

Just before serving, heat stuffed onions in 350-degree oven for about 10 minutes, until cheese in stuffing melts. Spoon butter sauce over and around onions when serving.

To serve on a buffet, have onions sliced through in half. Serves 12. One whole stuffed onion also can be served as a first course.

*Recipe adapted from Elizabeth on 37th Street Restaurant.

TOMATO PIE

1 9-inch pie shell, cooked and cooled
2 tablespoons Dijon mustard
About 4 peeled, sliced tomatoes
Salt and pepper to taste
4 ounces each white and yellow Cheddar cheese
2 tablespoons mayonnaise
3 tablespoons Parmesan cheese

When pie shell is cool, spread Dijon mustard on shell. Layer sliced tomatoes, salt and pepper and cheeses. End with cheese. For top layer, spread mayonnaise over cheese. Sprinkle with Parmesan. Bake at 350° until bubbly, about 20 minutes.

Cut into 8 wedges.

SHRIMP AND GRITS

4 cups coarse grits, prepared with half milk and half water, according to package directions

SHRIMP SAUCE

4 tablespoons butter
4 tablespoons flour

2 cups half-and-half
1 pound small shrimp, peeled and roughly chopped
1 tablespoon sherry
Pinch cayenne pepper
Salt and pepper to taste

Melt butter in saucepan. Whisk in flour. Cook over low heat for about 2 minutes. Add half-and-half slowly, whisking constantly. Cook over medium-low heat until mixture thickens. Add shrimp and allow to cook in sauce for about 10 minutes, until pink. Season to taste. Mixture can be refrigerated and reheated in microwave or on stovetop when ready to serve.

To serve, place grits in covered casserole. Have shrimp sauce in separate covered casserole. Serve sauce over grits.

CHEESE BLINTZ CASSEROLE

Filling:
   2 pounds cottage cheese
   2 eggs
   1/4 cup sugar
   Salt to taste
   Juice of 1 lemon
   1 teaspoon vanilla

Batter:
   1/2 cup sugar
   1 cup flour
   3 teaspoons baking powder
   Pinch salt
   2 sticks melted and cooled butter or margarine
   2 eggs
   1/4 cup milk
   1 teaspoon vanilla

Topping:
   1/4 cup sugar mixed with 2 teaspoons cinnamon

Garnish:
   Sour cream
   Strawberry or other preserves

Mix filling in large bowl and batter in small bowl. Place one-half of batter in 2-quart glass dish. Spread out evenly. Dabble filling on top and cover with remaining batter. Sprinkle with sugar/cinnamon mixture. Bake 40 minutes at 350°.
   Can freeze and reheat.
   Serve with sour cream and preserves.

FRESH FRUIT WITH BOILED DRESSING

Quantities to your liking:
   Fresh blueberries
   Pineapple chunks, canned or fresh
   Seedless grapes, purple or green
   Strawberries, whole or sliced
   Kiwifruit, peeled and sliced

Fruit Sauce:
   1 egg, beaten
   3/4 cup sugar
   Juice of 1 lemon, plus rind
   Juice of pineapple
   Juice of 1 orange

Boil sauce ingredients 1 minute. Stir well. Pour over fresh fruit. Sauced fruit keeps well in refrigerator for several days.

BREAKFAST YEAST RING

1/2 cup boiling water
1/2 cup solid shortening
7 tablespoons sugar
3/4 teaspoon salt
2 packages active dry yeast
1/2 cup lukewarm water
1/2 teaspoon sugar
1 egg
3 1/2 to 4 cups all-purpose flour

Topping:
   6 tablespoons melted butter

½ cup sugar
2 teaspoons cinnamon
½ cup chopped nuts

Frosting:
2 tablespoons butter
2 tablespoons milk
1½ to 2 cups confectioners' sugar

Garnish:
Pecan halves
Cherry halves

Pour boiling water over shortening. Add sugar and salt. Stir until well-mixed. Allow to cool. Combine yeast, ½ cup warm water and ½ teaspoon sugar. Allow yeast to activate (mixture will bubble up). Combine shortening mixture and yeast mixture. Add 1 egg. Mix well.

Gradually add flour, taking care not to add too much. Dough should be shiny and smooth. Cover dough and refrigerate 1 to 4 hours. Remove dough to lightly floured board. Divide in half. Roll half of dough into rectangular shape, ¼ inch thick. Spread with half of topping mixture. Roll up like jelly roll. Bring ends together, forming a ring. Place on greased cookie sheet. Using kitchen shears or knife, cut nearly through the roll at 1½-inch intervals. Twist slices sideways so filling shows.

Repeat with other half of dough, making a second ring.

Cover rings and allow to rise at room temperature, about 30 minutes to 1 hour. When double in size, bake at 350° for 10 minutes. Reduce to 300° and continue baking until lightly browned and thoroughly baked. Remove from oven and frost.

To make frosting: Combine butter, milk and sugar.

Spread hot ring with frosting. Garnish with chopped toasted pecans or whole toasted pecans and cherry halves.

Each ring serves 8 to 10. Freeze rings unfrosted. Frost after reheating at 300° for 20 minutes.

RIBS AT BEAULIEU

There was a time when you couldn't buy fresh herbs in the grocery stores in Savannah. Ashby Angell changed all that. "I like to cook and I couldn't buy them so I started growing them myself," she says. For 15 years, Ashby supplied restaurants with herbs, but now is content to grow them for fun in well-manicured beds surrounding her home on the Vernon River. Her husband, John, produces many of the vegetables Ashby uses in her innovative recipes.

Ashby created a casual spring menu that spotlights barbecued ribs, one of her son Charlie's specialties, and an array of colorful salads heavily accented with herbs and polished off with deep-dish apple pie—all served outside under the shade of a live oak with a view of the river and marsh to keep things down-to-earth, the way Ashby likes them.

Ribs and herbs have well-documented significance in Lowcountry cooking. Pork was the most prominent meat on Georgia tables in the 1850s and herbs were routinely grown on Lowcountry plantations. Seeds advertised for sale in Savannah newspapers between 1810 and 1825 included leeks, beets, asparagus, artichokes, nasturtium, marjoram, garlic, horseradish, mustard, sage, basil and savory. Georgians knew early on that fresh is best, as this menu illustrates.

GEORGIA CAVIAR

1 pound dried black-eyed peas
2 cups diced green pepper
1½ cups diced onion and green onion mixed, if desired
½ cup diced fresh jalapeño peppers (seeds removed)
1 2-ounce jar sliced pimientos, drained

Dressing:
⅓ cup red-wine vinegar
1 tablespoon balsamic vinegar
1 teaspoon salt
½ teaspoon freshly ground black pepper
1 tablespoon Dijon mustard
¼ teaspoon sugar
Pinch of dried basil or tarragon
½ cup olive oil
½ cup vegetable oil

MENU

•

BEER

GEORGIA CAVIAR WITH CORN CHIPS

BARBECUED RIBS

MARINATED GRILLED VEGETABLES
WITH PASTA AND PESTO

COLE SLAW WITH VINAIGRETTE

OLIVE COUNTRY BREAD WITH ROSEMARY

CREAM CHEESE POUNDCAKE
WITH PEACH ICE CREAM

OR

APPLE PIE WITH CRUMB TOPPING

Ribs should be about 3 inches across. If they are larger, have butcher cut them down the middle to make short ribs. Wash ribs. Pat dry. Combine sugar, pepper and salt in shaker jar and coat ribs with mixture. Allow to marinate at room temperature about 30 minutes.

Allow ribs to boil in red-wine vinegar and enough water to cover ribs. Boil until all fat cooks out, about 30 minutes.

Remove ribs from water. Add more dry marinade from shaker jar. Cook ribs over indirect heat over coals until they develop smoky flavor, about 30 minutes. Baste with red-wine vinegar and pepper mixture. You may add barbecue sauce the last 15 minutes, basting continuously. Cook ribs over direct heat the last few minutes, to brown.

Cut ribs before serving. Dribble sauce over all. Serve more sauce separately.

If serving ribs with accompaniments, as in this menu, you can reduce the amount of ribs to a half pound per person.

Soak peas in water for 6 hours, or overnight. Drain. Cook peas in large pan with water to cover for 40 minutes. Drain. Add peppers, onions and pimientos. Combine dressing ingredients. Add dressing until all vegetables are coated. Refrigerate overnight. Allow to come to room temperature. Taste. Serve with corn chips.

Serves 10 to 12, with chips.

RICHARD'S BARBECUE SAUCE

1 10-ounce can chicken broth
1 pint apple cider vinegar
1/2 bottle Heinz 57 sauce
1/4 bottle Texas Pete® hot sauce
1 tablespoon salt
1 tablespoon black pepper
1 teaspoon red pepper
1 stick butter
22 ounces ketchup

Combine ingredients. Simmer for 2 hours.

BARBECUED RIBS

1 pound of pork spareribs per person
2/3 cup sugar
2 tablespoons pepper
1 teaspoon salt
2 cups red wine vinegar

Basting sauce:
  Red wine vinegar
  Lots of black pepper

MARINATED GRILLED VEGETABLES WITH PASTA AND PESTO

1 small eggplant
1 small zucchini
1 yellow squash
Red and yellow sweet peppers
Onions: Vidalia, if available

Marinade:
  1/3 cup olive oil
  3 tablespoons lemon juice
  1/4 cup chopped onions
  1/4 cup chopped fresh basil
  2 cloves garlic, minced
  3/4 teaspoon salt
  1 teaspoon fennel seeds, crushed
  Coarsely ground black pepper

Slice vegetables into small pieces, 1½ to 2 inches long.

Marinate for several hours. Drain. Grill vegetables in grill basket over medium high heat until done to taste.

Cook shaped pasta of your choice. Toss with olive oil, pesto (found on page 28), Parmesan cheese, chopped fresh basil and grilled vegetables.

Important: Do not serve cold. Serve warm or at room temperature.

Serves 10 to 12.

COLE SLAW WITH VINAIGRETTE

Balsamic Vinaigrette:
  1 part vinegar to 2 parts olive oil
  1/2 teaspoon Dijon mustard
  1/2 teaspoon salt
  1/4 teaspoon coarse black pepper

Mixed Vegetable Slaw:
  1/2 head each green and red cabbages, shredded
  1/2 head Chinese cabbage, shredded
  Several bunches of arugula
  1/4 cup chives, diced
  1/4 cup Vidalia or green onions, diced

Toss vegetables with vinaigrette just before serving.

Note: This holds up better when serving a crowd than a lettuce salad does, if you wait until the last minute to dress. Thinly sliced carrots, celery and sweet peppers are optional additions.

OLIVE COUNTRY BREAD WITH ROSEMARY

1 package dry yeast
1/2 cup warm water
1½ cups warm milk
2 tablespoons sugar
1/2 cup cornmeal, plus extra for baking sheet
3 tablespoons unsalted butter, softened
1 cup coarsely chopped onion
4 tablespoons coarsely chopped fresh rosemary
2/3 cup pitted Calamata olives, halved

2 teaspoons salt
1 tablespoon coarse ground pepper
2 cups whole wheat flour
3 to 3½ cups unbleached all-purpose flour

Stir yeast, water and milk and sugar together. Allow to sit until foamy.

Combine cornmeal, butter, onion, rosemary, olives, salt, pepper, whole wheat flour and 2 cups all-purpose flour. Add yeast mixture; beat well. Place dough on floured board and add remaining flour as necessary until dough is workable and non-sticky. Allow dough to rest for 10 to 15 minutes.

Knead until smooth and elastic, adding more flour if necessary to keep from sticking.

Allow dough to rise, covered, in lightly oiled bowl for about 1½ hours. Punch dough down. Divide in half. Shape into round loaves. Sprinkle baking sheet with a little cornmeal and place loaves on it. Cover with kitchen towel and let rise again, about 45 minutes.

Preheat oven to 350°. Bake until bread is well-browned, about 45 minutes. Remove from baking sheet and set on wire rack to cool. Makes 2 loaves.

Serves 10 to 12. Freezes well.

CREAM CHEESE POUNDCAKE

3 sticks butter, at room temperature
8 ounces cream cheese, at room temperature
3 cups sugar
6 large eggs
3 cups cake flour, sifted
1 teaspoon vanilla

Cream butter and cream cheese at medium speed for about 2 minutes. Add sugar gradually. Cream for 5 to 7 minutes at medium speed. Add vanilla, then one egg, beating just until blended. Continue alternately adding 1 egg and ½ cup flour until all flour is added. Pour mixture into a greased and floured 10-inch tube pan. Bake at 325° for about 1 hour and 15 minutes, or until wooden toothpick inserted comes out clean.

Cool in pan on wire rack 10 to 15 minutes. Remove from pan and allow to cool completely on rack.

Makes 12 to 16 servings, depending on size of slice.

PEACH ICE CREAM

4 eggs
2½ cups sugar, divided
Pinch salt
2 teaspoons almond extract
4 cups milk, heated
1 quart fully ripened peaches, mashed
½ lemon, juiced
2 cups whipping cream

Beat eggs. Add 1 cup sugar gradually, beating well, then salt and almond extract. Pour mixture into hot, but not boiling, milk. Cook on low heat, stirring, in double boiler until thick. Set aside to cool.

Mash peaches and add remaining 1½ cups sugar (if peaches are very sweet they may not need as much sugar). Stir in lemon juice. When custard is cool, add peaches and mix well. Add cream, stirring to blend well.

Freeze according to manufacturers' directions. Makes about 3 quarts. Can be frozen for several weeks. Allow to sit at room temperature 10 minutes or so before serving.

Serves 10 to 12.

Apple Pie with Crumb Topping

APPLE PIE WITH CRUMB TOPPING

1 ready-made pie crust
3 large tart apples
1/2 cup granulated sugar
Juice of 1 lemon
1 stick butter
1 cup brown sugar
1 cup flour
1/2 cup chopped pecans or other nuts

Peel and slice apples into pie crust. Cover with granulated sugar and lemon juice.

Cream butter and brown sugar. Work in flour and nuts with fork or fingers. Crumble topping over apples.

Bake at 300° for 30 minutes.

Serve warm. Top with whipped cream or vanilla ice cream, if desired.

Serves 8.

CURRIED SHRIMP LADIES' LUNCH

Very early on, Savannah's colonists began to form societies and clubs designed to promote their various interests. Such organizations continue to flourish, with invitations quietly extended from one friend to another, resulting in a number of sewing clubs, card clubs, wine clubs, literary clubs, riding clubs, hunting clubs, poetry groups, sailing clubs and so on. Some hold informal functions. Others entertain on a grand scale with elaborate dinners, provocative readings and black-tie attire.

Still popular today in polite society is the ladies' lunch, often a combination of "natives" and newcomers who play cards, sew or pull weeds together. This savory menu fits such a gathering. It is, likewise, appealing to the hostess because so much of it can be prepared in advance. A rich shrimp curry spills over rice. Side dishes include spicy green beans and a Southern favorite, piquant tomato aspic. Brittle Bread, a relatively new Savannah tradition, is tiresome to make, but always appreciated by guests. Charlotte Russe and Lace Cookies are perhaps one of Savannah's finest dessert duos.

MENU

•

TOMATO ASPIC

GREEN BEAN BUNDLES

SHRIMP CURRY

RICE RING

BRITTLE BREAD

CHARLOTTE RUSSE

LACE COOKIES

TOMATO ASPIC

1 small package lemon gelatin
½ package unflavored gelatin
2 cups tomato juice (or V-8® juice)
¼ cup vinegar
Salt and pepper to taste
1 tablespoon Worcestershire sauce

1 shake Tabasco® sauce
½ small onion, minced
¾ cup chopped celery
¼ cup chopped bell pepper
Chopped green olives

Heat 1 cup of tomato juice. Dissolve lemon gelatin and gelatin in juice. Add all other ingredients. Pour into individual molds or large mold sprayed with vegetable spray. Chill until firm.

To unmold, allow mold or molds to sit at room temperature for about 10 minutes. Gently run knife around edges. Unmold. If mold appears to be sticking, fill sink with hot water and dip bottom of mold into this for a few seconds.

GREEN BEAN BUNDLES

2 pounds fresh green beans
8 green onions
1 red pepper, cut into 1/4-inch strips
1/3 cup butter
1 clove garlic, finely chopped
1/2 teaspoon thyme
1/4 teaspoon white pepper
Salt

Cook beans in salted water for 3 minutes. Plunge into ice water to preserve bright green color. Drain. Blanche green onions for a few seconds in hot water. Pat dry. Cut onion from stem. Gather a serving-size bundle of beans. Tie with onion stem. Repeat with rest of beans. Slip red pepper slices under onion knot.

Place bean bundles in buttered baking dish. Melt butter in sauté pan and sauté garlic for 1 minute. Add thyme and pepper. Pour over beans. Cover and refrigerate until ready to prepare. Bring to room temperature. Bake at 375° for 7 to 10 minutes, until beans are of desired tenderness.

Serves 8.

SHRIMP CURRY

4 tablespoons butter
1 large yellow onion, chopped fine
1/2 cup apple, chopped fine
1/2 cup celery, chopped fine
1 1/2 cups water
2 tablespoons curry powder
3 pounds shrimp, cleaned and deveined
1 pint half-and-half

Sauté onion, apple and celery in butter. When wilted, add water. Let simmer until apple and celery are tender and most of the liquid has evaporated. Stir in curry powder. Add half-and-half. Cook gently until cream is reduced to sauce consistency. Refrigerate. When ready to serve, bring mixture to simmer and add shrimp. Simmer until shrimp are just pink. Do not overcook.

Next to curry, have small bowls of grated coconut, chutney, chopped almonds and pickle relish or other specialty relishes.

Serves 8.

RICE RING

Prepare 4 cups cooked rice according to package directions. Immediately before serving buffet, sprinkle finely chopped parsley evenly into a ring mold. Press rice into mold and unmold it immediately onto serving platter. Pour shrimp curry into middle of ring. Have additional curry in a gravy boat with ladle.

Makes 8 1/2 cup servings.

BRITTLE BREAD

2¾ cups all-purpose flour
¼ cup sugar
½ teaspoon salt
½ teaspoon baking soda
½ cup butter
8 ounces plain yogurt
Additional salt or sugar

Sift together flour, sugar, salt and soda. Cut butter into dry mixture until it is the size of small peas. Blend in yogurt. Or, add butter to dry ingredients in food processor and process. Add yogurt and pulse four or five times until mixture gathers into a ball.

Refrigerate until dough is very firm. Take marble-size pieces of dough and roll unto floured surface until paper thin. Sprinkle with sugar or salt.

Place on ungreased baking sheets. Bake at 400° for 5 to 8 minutes, until lighted browned and puffed in places.

Remove to waxed paper to cool. Pile all of cooled bread onto baking sheets. Turn off oven. Return brittle bread to warm oven to crisp, at least 1 hour.

Store in airtight container. Can be frozen.

CHARLOTTE RUSSE

1½ envelopes unflavored gelatin
½ cup cold water
1 cup sugar
1 quart heavy cream
3 tablespoons cooking sherry or rum
1 tablespoon juice from maraschino cherries, optional

Dissolve gelatin in cold water. Set bowl over pot of hot water until contents are dissolved. Add sugar. Stir. Whip cream until firm, but not stiff.

Pour whipped cream into gelatin mixture. Stir in sherry or rum. Allow to chill until almost set. Stir in cherry juice to make streaks in mixture, if using.

Pour into one large mold, or if serving individually, pour into long-stemmed glasses.

Serve cold with coffee and lace cookies.

Serves 8.

Note: The late Sally Sullivan, a wonderful caterer, always lined a glass bowl with unfilled ladyfingers, and then filled the bowl with Charlotte. This makes for another lovely presentation.

LACE COOKIES

½ cup butter
¾ cup sugar
1 egg
1 teaspoon vanilla
3 tablespoons flour
½ teaspoon salt
1 cup quick-cooking oatmeal

Cream butter and sugar. Add egg and vanilla. Add flour, salt and oatmeal, mixing well. Drop by teaspoonsfuls onto foil-lined pans. Bake at 350° for 5 to 8 minutes, until lightly browned. Let cool before peeling from foil.

Makes about 2½ dozen. Cookies freeze well.

ELIZABETH TERRY'S TYBEE PORCH SUPPER

Savannah has her share of national celebrities. One of them is Elizabeth Terry, who came quietly to town in 1980 with her lawyer husband, Michael, and daughters Alexis and Celeste, renovated a 6,000-square-foot, turn-of-the-century mansion, and started cooking. Today, her restaurant—Elizabeth on Thirty Seventh —is paid for, the staff is stable, the girls are grown, and Terry—aided by Michael, who went from lawyer to restaurant manager—has won just about every kudo the food world offers. Elizabeth on Thirty Seventh has been named one of *Food & Wine Magazine's* top 25 restaurants in America and was elected to *Nation's Restaurant News'* fine dining Hall of Fame. In 1995, Terry was named by the James Beard Foundation as a Great Regional Chef.

She describes her winning culinary style this way: "The cooking in this part of the country has been developed over so many years by serious entertainers and cooks and caring mothers and housekeepers and fathers that I find it easy to avoid the current trend of mixing other ways of cooking and concentrate instead on this marvelous Southern way of company cooking."

Terry was asked to produce a menu suitable for serving on a hot summer night on the porch of her beachhouse on Tybee Island. "This is a summer meal that could be done ahead and includes things vegetarians can eat. That's why it's light. Also, during the summer, people's palates are jaded, and they want different flavors. I think this menu provides that."

GREEN HERB AND GOAT CHEESE DIP WITH GREEN VEGETABLES

MENU

•

GREEN HERB AND GOAT CHEESE DIP
WITH GREEN VEGETABLES

PICKLED SHRIMP AND VIDALIA ONION

CHICKEN AND BLACK-EYED PEA SALAD
WITH HONEY AND MUSTARD DRESSING

PEPPER-PECAN BRIOCHE

GINGER POACHED PEACHES
WITH LEMON SHERBET
AND GINGERSNAPS

2 tablespoons green onions, minced

1 tablespoon fresh chives, minced

2 teaspoons fresh mint or basil, minced

2 teaspoons cider vinegar

2 tablespoons extra virgin olive oil

1 teaspoon fresh cracked pepper

4 ounces Montrachet-style goat cheese, crumbled

1 cup half-and-half cream

2 green bell peppers, sliced

1 bunch celery, cut into sticks

2 small zucchini, cut into circles

1 bunch green onions

In the bowl of a food processor, add the onion, chives, mint, vinegar, olive oil and pepper. Process briefly and add the crumbled cheese. With the motor running, slowly pour in the cream. Process until smooth. Refrigerate to combine the flavors and thicken the dip at least 30 minutes before serving.

Serve in a bowl surrounded by vegetables for dipping.

PICKLED SHRIMP AND VIDALIA ONION

1 tablespoon vegetable oil
1 tablespoon pickling spices [purchased from spice
  section of supermarket]
2 bay leaves, whole
1 1/2 cups Vidalia or Spanish onions, peeled and
  cut into 1/2-inch dice
1 pound large shrimp, peeled and deveined
1/4 cup apple cider vinegar
1 teaspoon spicy chili sauce, any brand
2 teaspoons kosher salt
1 teaspoon fresh thyme, minced
3 garden-fresh tomatoes, diced, core discarded

In a large sauté skillet over high heat, warm the oil. Add the spices and bay leaves and sauté for 1 minute. Add the onion and sauté until the onion is translucent, about 1 minute. Stir in the shrimp and sauté until just pink. Turn off heat. Pour over the vinegar and cool. Add chili sauce. Sprinkle with salt and thyme. Remove bay leaves and hard spices. Cover and refrigerate. Garnish with tomato wedges and serve.

Serves 6 as an appetizer.

CHICKEN AND BLACK-EYED PEA SALAD WITH HONEY MUSTARD DRESSING

The dressing:
 2 tablespoons honey
 2 tablespoons Dijon mustard
 2 teaspoons soy sauce
 1/4 cup balsamic vinegar
 1/2 cup extra virgin olive oil

The salad:
 5 skinless, boneless chicken breasts
 2 tablespoons vegetable oil
 1 teaspoon balsamic vinegar
 1 teaspoon fresh thyme, minced
 1 teaspoon fresh cracked black pepper
 1 tablespoon kosher salt
 1/2 cup celery heart, minced
 1 cup green onion, minced
 1/2 cup parsley, minced
 1/2 cup dried cranberries, minced
 5 cups salad greens, mixed
 1 15-ounce can black-eyed peas, rinsed and drained
 1/4 cup roasted salted peanuts, minced

For salad: Whisk together oil, vinegar, thyme and pepper in a non-corrosive shallow dish. Coat both sides of each breast with this marinade, cover and refrigerate for 30 minutes (up to 6 hours.)

Sauté chicken breasts in the marinade over medium heat in a sauté skillet, turning once, until cooked through. Sprinkle with salt, cool, dice and combine with the pan juices, celery, onion, parsley and cranberries. Refrigerate.

Dressing: Have ingredients at room temperature. In the bowl of a food processor, add honey, mustard, soy sauce and vinegar. Process briefly. With motor running, slowly add olive oil. Set aside, but do not refrigerate.

Just before serving, divide greens among six plates. Toss dressing with chicken and spoon the chicken salad on top of greens. Garnish with black-eyed peas and peanuts.

If serving on casual buffet, place greens on large platter. Top with chicken salad. Garnish with peas and peanuts.

Serves 6.

PEPPER-PECAN BRIOCHE

1 tablespoon active dry yeast
1 tablespoon sugar
¼ cup lukewarm water
½ cup melted butter (4 ounces)
½ teaspoon salt
2 cups all-purpose flour

⅓ cup pecans, toasted and chopped
1 teaspoon fresh cracked peppercorns
2 eggs, beaten lightly

In bowl of a mixer, add yeast, sugar and water. Stir to dissolve and allow the mixture to sit 10 minutes, until bubbles form. Add cooled melted butter, salt, flour, pecans, pepper and eggs. Mix with dough hook in a mixer, or with a wooden spoon by hand until the mixture is smooth, about 5 minutes. Place dough in a buttered large bowl and cover with a tea towel and allow to rise until double in bulk, 1 to 1½ hours, no longer.

Shape dough and place into buttered loaf pan. Cover and allow to rise 1 hour. Bake in preheated 400-degree oven for 25 minutes until golden. Cool on wire rack.

Slice and serve with fruit preserves. Freezes well.

GINGER POACHED PEACHES

6 fresh ripe peaches, peeled and diced
½ cup sugar
Two ¼-inch slices fresh ginger
¼ cup water
2 teaspoons grenadine
1 pint lemon sherbet
1 package Swedish gingersnaps

In medium skillet, combine sugar, ginger, water and grenadine. Over high heat, bring to a boil while stirring. Add peaches and bring back to boil, stirring constantly. Turn off heat and allow peaches to cool in the liquid. Discard the two ginger slices.

Serve in glass bowls topped with a dollop of lemon sherbet. Serve with crisp Swedish gingersnaps.

July 4th Fish Fry

Southerners have traditionally eaten a great deal of fish because it was so readily available from the salt water along the coast as well as from freshwater rivers, lakes and ponds. Although early cookbooks recommend that fish be boiled, stewed and baked, the fish fry probably developed as a way for Southerners to feed fish to large crowds.

In some parts of the South, the fish fry side dish of choice is potato salad; in others, it's french fries. But in Savannah, fried fish is usually served with grits and hush puppies, plenty of cole slaw and a big platter of vine-ripe, ruby-red tomatoes. July is the month for the summer's first green peanuts, so boiled peanuts often make their debut as a Fourth of July appetizer, served with Bloody Marys hot as a firecracker.

Boiled Peanuts

Wash raw peanuts thoroughly. Put peanuts in large pot and cover completely with water. Add about 1/4 box of salt per five pounds of peanuts. Boil peanuts until firm, but tender, about 1 hour. Check frequently to see that peanuts always remain covered with water.

When peanuts are desired tenderness (this is quite an individual thing), turn off heat. Allow peanuts to sit in salty water until they begin to sink. Taste every 10 minutes to prevent them from absorbing too much salt. Drain. Eat hot, at room temperature or chilled.

Herb's Bloody Marys

46 ounces V-8® juice
2 teaspoons black pepper
1 teaspoon salt
1 tablespoon Worcestershire sauce
1/2 large lemon, squeezed
8 ounces vodka, or more, to taste
1 tablespoon celery seed
4 shakes of Tabasco®

Pour juice into a large pitcher. Do not stir until after you have added pepper, salt and Worcestershire sauce. Add lemon, vodka, celery seed and Tabasco®. Stir. Pour over ice. Garnish with celery sticks or lime or lemon slices.

Menu
•
BOILED PEANUTS

HERB'S BLOODY MARYS

FRIED FISH

ELOISE'S TARTAR SAUCE

BAKED GARLIC CHEESE GRITS

TRADITIONAL COLE SLAW

HUSH PUPPIES

SLICED TOMATOES

LEMON MERINGUE PIE

FRIED FISH

Any kind of fish fillets: bass, trout, king mackerel steaks, etc. (Allow 1 or 2 fillets per person or, small fish with bone in, such as bream or mullet, allow 3 fish per person)

1 cup cornmeal
1/2 cup all-purpose flour
Salt and pepper
Oil for frying fish

Place cornmeal and flour in paper bag. Season with salt and pepper and shake well. Toss in several fish at a time and shake bag to coat fish with cornmeal mixture. Fish can be cooked indoors in a large, deep frying pan in about 3 inches of oil. Or, for large crowds, it is best to cook fish in a gallon of oil in a cast-iron fish cooker. Cook fish in hot oil until they are browned on all sides; time varies according to thickness of fish.

As each batch is completed, place fish on brown-paper lined baking sheets and place in 200-degree oven to keep warm until all are ready and can be served.

ELOISE'S TARTAR SAUCE

4 tablespoons finely minced onion
2 cups mayonnaise
1/2 cup sweet pickle relish
1 tablespoon dried parsley flakes
1 1/2 teaspoons dried dill weed
1/2 teaspoon Nature's Seasons®

Combine ingredients. Mix well. Cover and refrigerate. Keeps two weeks in refrigerator.

BAKED GARLIC CHEESE GRITS

1 cup regular grits, uncooked
4 cups water
2 teaspoons salt
1/2 cup butter or margarine
1 garlic clove, minced or pressed
1 tablespoon Worcestershire sauce
  Dash of hot sauce (optional)
8 ounces grated sharp Cheddar cheese
2 eggs, lightly beaten

Cook grits in salted water. Add butter, garlic, Worcestershire sauce, hot sauce (if using) and Cheddar cheese. Add a small amount of hot grits to eggs to temper them, then add eggs to rest of grits. Stir well.

Pour into buttered casserole and bake at 350° for 45 to 50 minutes, until set. If desired, top casserole with thin cheese slices in pattern, which will melt in the last few minutes of cooking.

Serves 8 to 10 as side dish.

TRADITIONAL COLE SLAW

1 medium head cabbage, grated or thinly sliced
1 cup mayonnaise
½ teaspoon salt, or to taste
½ teaspoon black pepper, or to taste

Combine cabbage and mayonnaise. Salt and pepper to taste.

Note: There are a number of variations for cole slaw. You can stir salt and pepper into mayonnaise and add 1 tablespoon vinegar and a teaspoon of sugar before mixing with cabbage. Some people also like to add about ⅓ cup sweet pickle cubes, with juice.

HUSH PUPPIES

Cornmeal used to batter fish
1 additional cup self-rising cornmeal mix
½ cup finely chopped onion
1 egg
Beer (or water) enough to make thick but smooth
  consistency (about 6 ounces)

Combine ingredients and stir well. Mixture should be the consistency of mush. Spoon by teaspoonfuls into hot fish grease and fry until they float and are brown on all sides, about 5 minutes.

LEMON MERINGUE PIE

1½ cups sugar
½ cup cornstarch
¼ teaspoon salt
1½ cups cold water
3 large lemons, juiced
5 egg yolks
2 tablespoons butter
3 teaspoons grated lemon rind
1 8-ounce can crushed pineapple, drained (optional)
1 deep-dish pie shell, baked

Meringue:
  5 egg whites
  ¼ teaspoon cream of tartar
  ½ cup sugar
  ½ teaspoon vanilla

Filling: Mix sugar, cornstarch and salt in saucepan. Add water and juice from lemons and cook over medium heat until mixture is very warm, stirring constantly. Remove 1 cup of warm mixture and add to beaten egg yolks. Return mixture to saucepan. Cook until very thick. Remove from heat.

Add butter and stir until melted. Add lemon rind, and pineapple, if using. Pour warm mixture into warm pie shell. Top with meringue.

Meringue: Beat egg whites, adding cream of tartar slowly. Beat until foamy. Slowly add sugar, beating until stiff. Add vanilla. Spread meringue over filling, taking care to seal edges of meringue to all edges of crust.

Bake meringue-topped pie for 12 minutes at 350°. Allow to sit at room temperature. Serve same day for best results.

Makes 8 servings.

Note: Blueberry Crumble or Peach Cobbler (See Savory Summer Meal) would make an equally good ending to this meal.

SUPPER AT SEA

In Chatham County, there are 400 miles of navigable waters, which not only support a thriving international shipping business but provide a natural playground for those who want to fish, crab, shrimp, ski or simply take in the view. There are an estimated 15,000 registered boats in the county, and those residents lucky enough to have some sort of seaworthy craft often spend long summer days—early evening is a particularly magical time—out on the water.

Savannah's rivers are part of the Intracoastal Waterway, an inland water highway that runs from Maine to Key West and is maintained by the United States Corps of Engineers. The waterway is protected along the Georgia coast by a chain of barrier islands—Tybee, Ossabaw, Wassaw, Blackbeard, Sapelo, St. Catherine's, St. Simons, Jekyll and Cumberland— which buffer boaters and island communities from coastal storms. The barrier islands are significant, too, because they are on the Atlantic Flyway, offering shelter to migrating waterfowl. They also serve as a habitat for a number of other rare and endangered coastal birds and animals.

Most importantly, the barrier islands protect Georgia's 700,000 acres of salt marshes, mud flats and swamps that are home to many species of marine life. The marshes, which are emptied and filled every 12 hours with six to eight foot tides, are the beginning of an ecological web that starts with decaying marsh grass, which is eaten by hungry fiddler crabs, which are eaten by fish, crab, shrimp and fish, which are enjoyed by us humans.

Here's a meal that can be savored while contemplating the beauty of it all. You'll need a large cooler to keep things chilled.

MENU

•

SPICY HAM LOAF WITH
HORSERADISH CREAM

MOLDED CRABMEAT RING

FRESH FRUIT BOWL

TOMATO HERB MUFFINS

FUDGE BROWNIE MUFFINS

SPICY HAM LOAF WITH HORSERADISH CREAM

1½ tablespoons gelatin
¾ cup water
½ cup fresh lemon juice
2 tablespoons Worcestershire
   sauce
2 cups ground cooked ham
2 tablespoons mayonnaise
1 tablespoon horseradish
2 tablespoons chopped pimiento
¼ teaspoon Dijon mustard
⅛ teaspoon ground cloves
⅛ teaspoon ground nutmeg

1/2 teaspoon seasoned salt
1/8 teaspoon cayenne pepper

In a bowl, sprinkle the gelatin over 1/4 cup of water. Do not stir. Let gelatin soften until it has absorbed all of the water. In small saucepan, over high heat, combine remaining 1/2 cup of water with lemon juice and heat just to the boiling point. Stir the hot water/lemon juice mixture into softened gelatin until thoroughly dissolved. Add the Worcestershire sauce. Chill the mixture in the refrigerator until slightly thickened. Stir in the ham, mayonnaise, horseradish, pimiento, mustard and spices. Mix well. Pour mixture into small greased loaf pan, and chill until firm. Unmold and cut into thin slices.

Ice loaf with Horseradish Cream as if icing a cake. Serve with bland crackers.

Serves 8.

HORSERADISH CREAM

1/2 cup heavy cream, whipped
1 tablespoon prepared horseradish
1 tablespoon fresh lemon juice
Dash salt

Into whipped cream, gently fold the horseradish, lemon juice and salt.

MOLDED CRABMEAT RING

1 10-ounce can cream of mushroom soup
6 ounces softened cream cheese
2 tablespoons unflavored gelatin
1/2 cup white wine

1/2 cup finely chopped green onion
1/2 cup finely chopped Vidalia onion
1 cup finely chopped celery
1 pound white crabmeat
1 cup mayonnaise
1 teaspoon Tabasco
1 teaspoon salt
2 tablespoons lemon juice
1 tablespoon Worcestershire sauce®
1/2 teaspoon pepper
1 2-ounce jar pimiento

In top of a double boiler, heat soup over moderate heat. Add cream cheese. Blend with whisk. Dissolve gelatin in wine. Add to cream cheese mixture. Add remaining ingredients and fold together gently, so as not to break up crab. Pour into well-greased 8-inch ring mold or spring mold. Cover and refrigerate overnight, or at least several hours. Unmold by wrapping mold with hot towel for a minute. Garnish with pimientos.

Serves 8.

FRESH FRUIT BOWL

1 cantaloupe, scooped out with melon baller
1 cup fresh blueberries, whole
1 pint fresh strawberries, washed and sliced
1 cup white grapes, whole
3 tablespoons lemon juice
1 tablespoon powdered sugar
Fresh mint for garnish

Combine lemon juice and powdered sugar. Stir into fruit. Serve in large bowl. Garnish with fresh mint.
Serves 8.

In large bowl, stir together flour, baking powder, salt and pepper. In medium bowl, whisk together milk, egg and olive oil. Add cheese, tomatoes, onions and herbs to dry mixture. Combine wet and dry ingredients; stir just till blended.

Spoon into prepared muffin tins, filled three-fourths full. Bake at 375° until a toothpick inserted in center of muffins comes out clean, about 20 minutes. Cool in tins for 3 minutes. Remove.

Makes 12 muffins.

Serve with Tomato-Herb Butter: Combine butter and about a tablespoon of tomato paste, along with finely chopped fresh herbs of your choice—basil, tarragon or rosemary.

TOMATO HERB MUFFINS

2 cups all-purpose flour
1 tablespoon baking powder
1/2 teaspoon salt
1/4 teaspoon freshly ground pepper
1 cup milk
1 egg
1/4 cup olive oil
1/2 cup freshly grated Parmesan cheese
1/4 cup finely chopped fresh tomatoes, drained
1/4 cup finely chopped Vidalia onions,
  sautéed in butter until limp
2 teaspoons fresh herbs—basil, tarragon
  or rosemary, finely chopped

FUDGE BROWNIE MUFFINS

1/2 cup butter or margarine
3 tablespoons unsweetened cocoa powder
2 large eggs, lightly beaten
1 cup sugar
1 teaspoon vanilla extract
3/4 cup all-purpose flour
1/4 cup finely chopped pecans, toasted
Semisweet chocolate morsels

Melt butter. Add cocoa. Combine eggs, sugar and vanilla extract. Beat well. Add butter mixture, flour and chopped pecans, stirring until just blended.

Spoon into large muffin cups that have been sprayed with vegetable spray, filling three-fourths full. Sprinkle tops of each muffin with a few chocolate morsels. Bake at 350° for 20 minutes. Remove from pans immediately and cool on wire rack.

Makes 10. Muffins freeze well.

SAVORY SUMMER MEAL

Crabbing is one of the most satisfying of all Lowcountry pursuits. Atlantic blue crabs are caught in the summer and fall in the tidal creeks that finger their way through the marsh grass. Crabbing with hand lines provides the most sport. Chicken necks or backs are pinned onto a length of twine and lowered over the sides of small boats into the salt water. The crabs, swimming by as the tide empties and then refills the creeks, latch onto the chicken necks with great vigor. The crabber cautiously pulls the line in until the crab is just beneath the surface of the water, where it can be scooped up with a shallow net and deposited into a five gallon bucket. On a good day, one can easily catch six or seven dozen crabs.

At home, the crabs are boiled, picked and eaten with butter. It's a messy, laborious, finger-licking task. Use the leftover picked meat in some delicacy, such as these crab cakes. (A dozen crabs yields about a pound of meat. You can also buy crabmeat by the pound.)

In fact, this meal represents some of the best reasons to be in Savannah in late summer: a smooth shrimp butter served with crackers, a cool Vidalia onion vichyssoise, followed by crab cakes served with a colorful stir fry of zucchini, squash, peppers and tomatoes from the garden, flavored with fresh herbs. We've offered two variations for peach cobbler—a quick and a traditional version—as well as a blueberry cobbler. Whichever dessert you choose, serve it hot, with vanilla ice cream.

MENU

•

RUM PUNCH

SHRIMP PASTE

VIDALIA ONION VICHYSSOISE

HEARTS OF PALM SALAD

CRAB CAKES WITH LEMON DILL SAUCE

SUMMER VEGETABLE STIR-FRY

CHEESE BISCUITS

PEACH COBBLER

OR

BLUEBERRY CRUMBLE WITH
ICE CREAM

RUM PUNCH

Per drink:
   2 ounces dark rum
   1 ounce cranberry juice
   1 ounce pineapple juice
   1/8 teaspoon maraschino
      cherry juice
   1/2 to 1 tablespoon fresh
      lime juice
   Lemons to float in drink

Combine ingredients. Increase amounts according to number of guests.

SHRIMP PASTE

2 pounds shrimp, cooked and
   cleaned
1/2 cup butter, softened

Shrimp Paste

1/2 teaspoon lemon juice
2 tablespoons mayonnaise
1 teaspoon Worcestershire sauce
Salt and black pepper to taste

Chop shrimp in food processor; do not overprocess. Add remaining ingredients and blend by hand. Mold in 3-cup mold, greased lightly with mayonnaise. Serve with bland crackers.
    Serves 8 to 10.

VIDALIA ONION VICHYSSOISE

3 medium leeks, white part only, cleaned well and sliced
1 Vidalia onion, chopped
2 tablespoons butter
2 baking potatoes, peeled and sliced
2 cups chicken broth
1 cup half-and-half
1 1/4 cups heavy cream

Salt to taste
Chives to garnish

Cook leeks and onion in butter. Add potatoes and broth. Simmer 30 minutes. Purée. Add half-and-half. Cool. Salt to taste. Pour in heavy cream just before serving. Combine well.
    Serves 8.

HEARTS OF PALM SALAD

1 bunch Romaine lettuce, washed
  torn into bite-sized pieces
1 14 1/2-ounce can artichoke hearts, drained, trimmed
  of tough leaves and quartered
4 ounces mushrooms, sliced
1 can hearts of palm, sliced 1/4-inch thick
Homemade garlic croutons

Combine salad ingredients. Just before serving, toss well with dressing.
    To make croutons: Cut French bread into cubes. Toast in oven until light brown. Sauté in frying pan with approximately 2 tablespoons of olive oil and 1 clove minced or pressed garlic.
    Serves 8.

LEMON VINAIGRETTE

1 clove garlic, minced or pressed
1/3 cup red-wine vinegar
Juice of 1 lemon
1 teaspoon salt
1/2 teaspoon freshly ground pepper

1 teaspoon dry mustard
Tabasco® to taste
1 teaspoon Dijon mustard
1/4 teaspoon sugar
Pinch dried tarragon
Pinch dried basil
1/2 cup olive oil
1/2 cup vegetable oil

Combine ingredients in shaker bottle. Shake well. If refrigerated, allow to come to room temperature before serving.

CRAB CAKES WITH LEMON DILL SAUCE

1 tablespoon butter
1 green onion, finely chopped
1 clove garlic, pressed
2 tablespoons red bell pepper, finely chopped
Cayenne pepper to taste
3 tablespoons heavy cream
1 tablespoon Dijon mustard
1 egg
1/2 teaspoon minced parsley
1/2 cup bread crumbs
1 pound white or claw crab meat, picked through
  for shells

Topping:
1/2 cup bread crumbs
1/4 cup grated Parmesan cheese
2 tablespoons oil
2 tablespoon butter

Sauté onion, garlic and bell pepper in butter until pepper is limp, about 3 minutes. Add cayenne, cream and mustard. Mix well. Add egg, parsley, and bread crumbs. Mix well. Gently fold in crab.

Form into eight patties, about 1/2 inch thick. Combine bread crumbs and Parmesan cheese. Pat topping onto both sides of patties. Refrigerate until firm, about 2 hours.

Combine oil and butter in heavy-bottomed or electric skillet. Sauté crab cakes in hot oil/butter mixture for about 3 minutes on each side. Or, place patties on cookie sheet. Dribble with oil and butter mixture. Bake at 400° for 7 to 10 minutes.

Serve with lemon dill sauce.

Makes 8.

LEMON DILL SAUCE

1 cup mayonnaise
¼ cup buttermilk
2 tablespoons chopped fresh dill
1 tablespoon minced parsley
2 teaspoons lemon juice
1 tablespoon grated lemon peel
1 small garlic clove, minced

Combine ingredients. Chill. Mixture will thicken as it chills. Place a dollop beside crab cakes. Pass extra sauce.

SUMMER VEGETABLE STIR-FRY

2 zucchini, pared lightly and sliced into ¼-inch rounds
1 or 2 yellow squash, sliced into ¼-inch rounds
1 large onion, cut in eighths
1 large green pepper, cut in strips
1 large red pepper, cut in strips
1 large yellow pepper, cut in strips
1 garlic clove, minced
2 tablespoons olive oil
1 1-pound can whole tomatoes, roughly chopped,
  with juice
3 tablespoons parsley, washed and chopped
1 tablespoon fresh dill, chopped
1 tablespoon fresh basil, chopped
¼ cup Parmesan cheese, grated

In large stir-fry pan, saute zucchini, squash, onion, peppers and garlic in olive oil until vegetables begin to soften, about 5 minutes. Add tomatoes and juice.

Sprinkle on herbs. With pan uncovered, allow mixture to cook about 10 minutes more. Turn off heat. Sprinkle on Parmesan cheese.
  Serves 8.

CHEESE BISCUITS

3 cups self-rising flour
1 cup solid shortening
½ pound sharp Cheddar cheese, grated
1 cup buttermilk

Combine flour and shortening in food processor, or cut shortening into flour with two knives, scissor-fashion. Mix in cheese. Add buttermilk. Stir gently just until ingredients are combined. Batter will be quite moist. Drop by spoonful onto non-stick baking sheet. Bake at 400° for 10 minutes.
  Serves 8.

QUICK PEACH COBBLER

½ cup butter or margarine
1 cup self-rising flour
1 cup milk
1 cup sugar
2 cups sliced fresh peaches, with juice

Melt butter in glass 9-x-13-inch pan. Mix flour, milk and sugar. Pour batter over melted butter. Do not stir. Add peaches and juice, distributing evenly. Do not stir. Bake at 350° for 35 to 40 minutes, until browned.
  Serves 8.

1 cup water
1/2 cup butter, melted
1 teaspoon almond extract

In bowl, mix well flour and salt. Cut in shortening. Pour boiling water over. Mix well with pastry cutter until forms ball.

Line a 9-x-13-inch pan with half of crust. Fill with peaches. Mix flour, sugar, cinnamon, water, melted butter and extract. Pour over peaches. Cover with other half of crust. Pinch edges of bottom and top crusts together. Bake at 350° for 1 hour.

Serves 14 to 16.

Note: Cooked cobbler freezes well. Halve crust and filling and make one smaller cobbler if desired.

TRADITIONAL PEACH COBBLER

Pastry:
 3 1/2 cups flour
 2 teaspoons salt
 1 1/2 cups shortening
 1/2 cup boiling water

Filling:
 8 cups sliced fresh peaches
 1/3 cup flour
 2 cups sugar
 1 teaspoon ground cinnamon

BLUEBERRY CRUMBLE

1 pint blueberries
2 tablespoons lemon juice
1/3 cup sugar

Topping:
 3/4 cup flour
 1/4 teaspoon salt
 1/3 cup sugar
 1/3 cup margarine or butter

Combine blueberries, lemon juice and sugar. Place in ungreased pan. Combine flour, salt and sugar. Cut in margarine to make crumbly topping. Crumble over top of blueberries. Bake at 350° for 35 minutes.

Serves 6.

A Symphony-In-The-Park Picnic

James Edward Oglethorpe, Savannah's founder, laid out Georgia's first colony as a series of wards and squares. The squares provided safety for the citizens if Savannah was attacked, and also served as the social hub of the town. Subsequent leaders expanded Oglethorpe's design, and by the mid-1800s, there were 24 squares in all, with a large park—Forsyth—developed at the end of Bull Street in 1851. Through the years, some of the squares were lost, but today, 21 of the original 24 have been restored. They are the heart and soul of downtown Savannah, each with its own name and its own horticultural design, many with monuments to important contributors to Savannah's history.

Forsyth Park is the largest and most spectacular of Savannah's parks. It encompasses 31 acres of walkers, runners and park-bench sitters, as well as scampering squirrels, soaring pigeons, squealing children and athletes tossing and catching Frisbees™, running down soccer balls or swinging tennis rackets. The park is surrounded by live oaks laden with Spanish moss and is lush with greenery: azaleas, camellias, Indian hawthorn, yaupon holly, magnolia, sabal palm, crape myrtle and dogwood. At the center of the park is a grand, cast-iron fountain erected in 1858 and renovated by citizens in 1988.

Every fall, as many as 5,000 Savannahians come to Forsyth Park with their blankets, lawn chairs and coolers to hear the Savannah Symphony Orchestra perform an outdoor concert sponsored by the city. This citywide concert in the park, begun in 1978, has created another occasion for Savannahians to become culinarily creative. Tablecloths are spread, candles are lit, prizes are given and almost anywhere in the park is said to be the best seat in the house.

This menu is a melody of intense flavors and colors: cream cheese spiked with herbs; tenderloin basted with a dry marinade before baking or grilling; a broccoli, onion, bacon and raisin salad; and potato salad made with skin-on new potatoes and creamy horeradish sauce. Strawberries and lemon squares are a fitting finale. You'll need two coolers: one for the cold stuff and a smaller one to keep the tenderloin warm.

Menu

•

Herbed Cream Cheese
with Crackers

Beef Tenderloin

Horseradish Potato Salad

Broccoli Salad with Sweet
and Sour Dressing

Strawberries and Powdered Sugar

Lemon Squares

Suggested Wine:
*A Southern French wine less full-bodied,
such as Chateauneuf-du-Pape
or a California merlot*

HERBED CREAM CHEESE

8 ounces cream cheese, softened
1/2 cup unsalted butter, softened
1 garlic clove, minced or pressed
1 teaspoon dried oregano
1/2 teaspoon dried thyme
1/2 teaspoon dried basil
1/2 teaspoon freshly ground black pepper

Combine ingredients in mixer or food processor. Store in covered crock in refrigerator. Chill at least 24 hours before serving. Serve at room temperature with crackers or veggie sticks, such as carrots and celery.

Makes 1 1/2 cups.

BEEF TENDERLOIN

1 5-pound beef tenderloin
1/4 teaspoon garlic salt
1/4 teaspoon celery salt
1/4 teaspoon onion salt
Juice of 1 lemon

Combine salts with lemon juice. Rub this mixture into meat. Allow to sit in covered glass dish in refrigerator overnight. Grill meat over hot coals about 30 minutes, or until thickest portion registers 140° on a meat thermometer. Or, roast in oven 15 minutes at 550°, reduce temperature to 350° and continue roasting for 20 minutes. (Meat will be very pink in the middle and less pink on the ends. Roast additional 10 minutes if meat is too rare.) Wrap well in foil and keep warm in small cooler.

Serves 6 as a main course.

HORSERADISH POTATO SALAD

1 1/2 cups mayonnaise
1 8-ounce carton sour cream
1 1/2 teaspoons horseradish, or more to taste
1 teaspoon celery seed
8 medium potatoes, cooked, peeled and sliced (if using new potatoes, clean, but do not peel)
1 cup parsley, washed, dried and chopped
3/4 cup chopped green onions
Additional parsley and onions for garnish

Combine mayonnaise, sour cream, horseradish and celery seed. Set aside. Place half of the potatoes in a medium bowl; sprinkle with 1/3 cup parsley and 1/4 cup onion. Spread on half of mayonnaise mixture. Do not stir. Repeat layers, ending with a layer of mayonnaise mixture that completely covers top of potatoes. Garnish with remaining parsley and onion. Cover with plastic wrap. Chill.

When ready to serve, stir mixture together.

Serves 8 to 10.

Note: Can be made up to 12 hours ahead of serving time. Add ½ teaspoon salt and pepper if desired.

BROCCOLI SALAD WITH SWEET AND SOUR DRESSING

Dressing:
  1 large whole egg
  ½ cup sugar
  ½ teaspoon dry mustard
  1½ teaspoons cornstarch
  ¼ cup white vinegar
  ⅓ cup water
  ¼ teaspoon salt
  2 tablespoons butter or margarine, softened
  ¾ cup mayonnaise

Salad:
  4 cups raw broccoli florets
  1 cup raisins
  1 cup sliced mushrooms
  ½ cup chopped purple onion
  4-6 slices bacon, cooked crisp and crumbled

For dressing, whisk together egg, sugar, mustard and cornstarch. In saucepan, combine vinegar, water and salt. Bring to a boil. Whisk in egg mixture and cook about 1 minute, or until thickened, whisking constantly. Remove pan from heat and whisk in butter. Add mayonnaise; stir. Chill dressing in covered container.

To make salad: Combine salad ingredients. Pour dressing over. Toss well. Salt and pepper to taste. Serve within several hours. If salad sits, drain off any liquid that accumulates, and retoss.

Serves 6 to 8.

LEMON SQUARES

1 cup butter, melted
2 cups plus 4 tablespoons all-purpose flour
1 cup powdered sugar
4 eggs
2 cups granulated sugar
1 teaspoon baking powder
Grated rind of 2 lemons
6 tablespoons fresh lemon juice (about 2 lemons)
Additional confectioners' sugar for dusting squares

Combine butter, 2 cups flour and 1 cup powdered sugar with wooden spoon. Pat with floured hands into buttered 9-by-13-inch baking pan. Bake at 350° for 20 minutes.

While crust is cooling, beat together eggs, sugar, baking powder, rind, remaining flour and lemon juice. Pour over baked crust and bake at 350° for an additional 30 to 35 minutes, until filling is brown.

Cool, then sprinkle lightly with confectioners' sugar. Trim edges, then cut into bars.

Makes 24 large bars. Freezes well.

THE LOWCOUNTRY BOIL

One of Savannah's favorite casual parties is probably the one we can least lay claim to. The Lowcountry Boil—a one pot dish that can include sausage, corn, shrimp, crab, new potatoes, golf ball sized onions and even carrots boiled together in seasoned water and dumped on a table or in a huge decorative bowl for all to enjoy—is a dish originally claimed by South Carolina, where it is commonly called Frogmore Stew, Geechee Boil or Dump It.

But never mind. Savannah has adopted the dish as its own, and with good reason. It showcases sausage, once the mainstay of the Southern diet, the freshest corn, grown in profusion in the area, and local shrimp, at their peak in July, August and September.

Trish McLeod, who has been catering since 1987, explains this rather elaborate outdoor menu: "I am always looking for something different, which is why I include some of the other foods in addition to the Lowcountry Boil. Basically, I want good-tasting, good-looking, very fresh food." You could certainly pare down the offerings, serving just the Lowcountry Boil, green salad and chocolate bark.

Plan this party when the moon is full and the tide is high. Have guests gather late in the day, and send the teen-agers off to water-ski while the adults sip Burma Bombs or beer, pick boiled crab, and munch raw veggies. Serve the Lowcountry Boil and accompaniments as the sun is dipping beneath the horizon.

MENU
•
BURMA BOMB

BOILED CRAB

CRUDITÉS WITH HERB DIP

PASTA WITH PARSLEY-BASIL PESTO

LOWCOUNTRY BOIL

RED RICE

GRILLED MUSTARD CHICKEN

GREEN SALAD WITH LEMON-GINGER VINAIGRETTE

CHOCOLATE BARK

BURMA BOMB

Per Drink:
1½ ounces Bacardi® Gold Rum (Ronrico)
6 ounces Fresca® or ginger ale or tonic
2-3 splashes Pink Grapefruit Juice Cocktail or orange juice
Sprigs of mint

Combine liquid ingredients. Serve over ice with sprigs of mint as garnish.

BOILED CRAB

Fill 20-gallon kettle half full of water. Add 2 tablespoons (or more) Old Bay® seasoning. Bring water to boil. Add live crabs. Place lid on top.

Boil crabs vigorously for 15 minutes. Remove from water and allow to cool before picking.

CRUDITÉS WITH HERB DIP

Leave all vegetables raw, except asparagus. To blanch asparagus, plunge spears into boiling water. Allow to boil 2 to 5 minutes, depending on size of spears and taste preference. Drain immediately. Plunge cooked asparagus into sink of ice water to stop cooking and preserve color. Drain immediately.

Favorite raw vegetables:
  Sliced carrots
  Sliced celery
  Snowpeas or sugar snaps
  Red and yellow bell pepper strips
  Cauliflower, broken into florets
  Whole mushrooms, cleaned with brush or damp
    paper towel

Dip
  1 cup mayonnaise
  1/2 cup sour cream
  1/4 cup chopped parsley
  1 tablespoon grated onion
  Capers to taste
  Freshly chopped chives to taste
  1/2 tablespoon lemon juice
  1/2 teaspoon Worcestershire sauce
  1/4 teaspoon paprika
  1/4 teaspoon curry powder

Process in food processor. Makes about 1½ cups.

PASTA WITH PARSLEY-BASIL PESTO

2-3 cloves garlic
1 cup parsley leaves, packed
1 cup basil leaves, packed
1/2 cup pecans, walnuts or pine nuts
1/3 cup olive oil or more to bind
3/4 cup (or more) freshly grated Parmesan
Salt and pepper
3/4 pound long or short pasta noodles, cooked al dente

In food processor, with motor running, drop in cloves of garlic. Add parsley leaves, basil leaves and nuts of your choice. Slowly add olive oil and process until mixture holds together. Add Parmesan, salt and pepper to taste. Toss with warm pasta. Serve at room temperature.

Serves 8. For party for 35 to 40, make four recipes pesto and toss with 3 to 3½ pounds dried pasta, cooked al dente.

LOWCOUNTRY BOIL

8 medium onions, cut in half
Corn—about ½ ear per person, cut into 1-inch pieces
14 pounds large raw shrimp
2-3 small new potatoes per person
¼ pound per person kielbasa Polish sausage
2 lemons, sliced
Old Bay® seasoning, to taste

Allow 1 hour to heat water in 20-gallon pot, filled about one-third full. About 45 minutes before serving, add lemon slices, seasoning, new potatoes and sausage.

About 30 minutes before serving, add onion. Add corn about 15 minutes before serving. Ten minutes before serving, add shrimp. When shrimp turn pink and are cooked through (10 minutes or less), drain contents. Serve hot.

Serves 35 to 40.

bell pepper and cook until about half done. Add rice and sauté a few minutes. Add juices and bring to a boil, stirring constantly. Add sugar, baking soda, salt and pepper. Lower heat to low and cook until liquid is about half gone. Pour rice mixture into several casseroles. Cover. Bake about 25 minutes at 350°. Uncover and cook more if not all of moisture has evaporated, about 10 minutes. Stir in cooked bacon just before serving.

Serves 35 to 40.

Note: Rice will be slightly crunchy. Best if cooked close to the time it is to be served. May also be cooked in advance, refrigerated, and microwaved on high, covered with paper towel.

RED RICE

8 strips bacon, chopped
6 cups raw rice
2 cups onions, chopped into 1/2-inch pieces
3/4 cup green bell pepper, chopped into 1/2 inch pieces
1 teaspoon sugar
1/8 teaspoon baking soda
5 1/4 cups each V-8® and tomato juices
Salt and pepper to taste

Sauté bacon until crisp. Remove and reserve. In bacon drippings, sauté onions until about half cooked. Add

GRILLED MUSTARD CHICKEN

6 boneless, skinless chicken breasts, washed and thick
  end flattened
4 tablespoons coarse mustard
1/4 cup lemon juice
1/8 cup water or 1 tablespoon oil and 1 tablespoon water
1-3 cloves minced garlic (to taste)
4 dashes Worcestershire sauce
Fresh black pepper to taste

Combine ingredients. Marinate chicken breasts for at least one hour, refrigerated, in mixture. Grill over hot coals about 15 minutes, until chicken is cooked through. Thinly slice.

Serves 12, with other items. To feed 35 to 40, allow 1/2 breast per person and increase marinade four times.

GREEN SALAD WITH LEMON-GINGER VINAIGRETTE

Mixed greens (Romaine, Boston, spinach and
leaf lettuce), about ¾ packed cup per person
70 stalks asparagus, blanched and sliced into 2-inch
pieces
70 sugar snap peas, raw
35 raw mushrooms, sliced
5 cups homemade croutons
½ cup grated Parmesan
Salt
Freshly ground pepper

Serves 35 to 40.

LEMON-GINGER VINAIGRETTE

2 tablespoons fresh lemon juice
¼ cup olive oil
1 clove garlic
½ teaspoon each: salt, sugar, grated lemon rind,
grated fresh ginger

Combine salad ingredients. Toss with salad. To dress salad for 35 to 40, make five recipes of dressing.

HOMEMADE CROUTONS: Cut French bread into cubes ½ by ¾ inches. Add liquid margarine, enough to coat bread cubes. Sprinkle lightly with garlic salt. Bake in 325-degree oven about 30 to 45 minutes, until very dry and crunchy, stirring frequently. Store in plastic bags. Can be frozen.

CHOCOLATE BARK

1 stack of saltine crackers
1 cup light brown sugar, packed
1 cup (2 sticks) margarine
1 12-ounce package semi-sweet chocolate morsels
Finely chopped pecans (optional)

Line a 10-x-15-inch baking sheet with heavy duty aluminum foil. Lay crackers on foil in solid layer, edges touching. Boil margarine and brown sugar for 3 minutes, stirring constantly. Pour over crackers, spreading to cover them all. Bake at 400° for 5 to 7 minutes, checking to see that mixture does not burn. Remove from oven. Allow to sit about 3 minutes. Sprinkle chocolate chips evenly over candy and spread with a spatula as chocolate begins to melt. Sprinkle nuts, if using, evenly over chocolate.

When cool, break into pieces. Store in refrigerator. Serves 10 to 15.

Note: Fresh strawberries or lemon squares (see Symphony-in-the-Park Picnic menu, page 73) are also good endings for this menu.

A GULLAH BOARD MEETING BUFFET

In early Savannah kitchens, African cooks had the job of transforming raw ingredients from land and sea into feasts for the bountiful tables set by Savannah's planters and merchants. These cooks were typically given verbal instructions by English mistresses, then were left to their own devices to create the requested dish. African traditions, naturally, crept into the traditionally English manner of cooking.

Many of the favorite dishes of early days in Savannah relied on ingredients cooks had grown up with in Africa—maize, peanuts, red peppers, rice, yams, okra, peas and sesame seeds, also called benne seeds. African cooks are credited with the creation of classic Lowcountry dishes such as pilau—rice and chicken, shrimp or oysters stewed together with stock—okra and tomatoes, and sweet potato pie.

Slaves along the South Carolina and Georgia sea islands created a special culture called Gullah, and spoke a thick, lilting mix of African and English, also called Gullah. The culture and language are vanishing rapidly today.

One organization keen on researching, recording and remembering the historic and cultural contributions of African-Americans is the Beach Institute African-American Cultural Center, located in one of the city's oldest black neighborhoods in downtown Savannah. On display at the Institute is a collection of carvings by the late Ulysses Davis, done in mahogany, cypress and pecan. Davis, who whittled between haircuts at the 45th Street barber shop he owned, carved the busts of America's 41 presidents, mythical beasts and costumed African tribal kings. The collection of 200 pieces is considered one of the most significant Southern folk-art collections in existence, the perfect backdrop, we felt, for this board meeting buffet featuring traditional dishes made famous by African-American cooks.

Important to this menu are the pilaus, often referred to as "per-lows" by slave cooks. Spicy devilled crab and sweet potato pie are still served on Friday and Saturday nights, along with ribs in a mustard sauce, at Wall's Barbecue, a mostly take-out restaurant operated by African-Americans on a dirt lane near the Beach Institute. Benne wafers, thin and buttery, are the natural conclusion to this salute to African-American taste traditions.

MENU

•

SPICY DEVILED CRAB

OKRA AND TOMATOES

FRIED CHICKEN

OYSTER PILAU

SHRIMP PILAU

CORN PONE

SWEET POTATO PIE

MRS. SULLIVAN'S BENNE WAFERS

SPICY DEVILED CRAB

¹/₂ cup Bloody Mary mix
4 tablespoons butter
10 saltines, finely crumbled
¹/₄ teaspoon dry mustard
¹/₂ teaspoon salt
¹/₈ teaspoon cayenne pepper
¹/₈ teaspoon black pepper
1 tablespoon Worcestershire sauce
1 additional tablespoon butter
2 tablespoons minced green onion
1 tablespoon minced red pepper
1 tablespoon minced celery
1¹/₂ pounds white or claw crab meat
8 to 10 crab shells

Topping:
  4 tablespoons butter
  Dry bread crumbs
  Paprika or cayenne pepper

Heat Bloody Mary mix. Add butter and stir to melt. Add crumbled saltines and seasonings. Sauté green onion, red pepper and celery in 1 tablespoon butter until limp, about 2 minutes. Add to Bloody Mary mixture. Carefully add crab meat and stir gently to combine. Pack in shells. Cover with bread crumbs lightly sautéed in butter.

Sprinkle cayenne pepper or paprika on top, depending on spiciness desired.

Bake at 350° for about 20 minutes, until heated through.

Or, wrap deviled crabs in plastic wrap and place in freezer bag. Freeze for up to six months. When ready to eat, bake frozen crabs at 350° for 40 minutes, until filling is hot and tops of deviled crab are brown.

Makes 8 to 10 deviled crabs. One crab is a perfect first course. If serving as a main meal, allow two per person.

OKRA AND TOMATOES

4 slices hickory-smoked bacon
1 large onion chopped
1 pound fresh okra, ends trimmed and sliced
5 ripe tomatoes, peeled and chopped, or 1 large can
  whole peeled tomatoes, chopped, with juice
Salt and cayenne pepper to taste
¹/₂ cup chicken broth

Sauté bacon until crisp. Remove bacon from skillet and crumble. Add onion to bacon grease and cook until soft, about 3 minutes. Add okra and sauté for a minute

Early in the day, season chicken with salt and pepper. Refrigerate. When ready to fry, toss chicken in bag with flour, a few pieces at a time, until each is coated with flour.

Heat oil in heavy, large skillet with lid. When hot, add chicken in single layer. Cover and cook on medium high for about 10 minutes. Remove cover, turn chicken to other side and continue cooking on medium high for about 10 more minutes. Remove smaller pieces first. Drain on brown paper bags or paper towels.

Serves 4 as a main dish. Serves 8 as part of a buffet. Good warm, at room temperature or cold.

OYSTER PILAU

6 to 8 slices bacon
1 medium onion, chopped fine
1/2 cup chopped green pepper
1/2 cup chopped celery
1 1/4 cups raw rice
2 cups oyster liquid and chicken stock
1 pint oysters

In large frying pan, cook bacon until crispy. Crumble and set aside. Add onions, celery and green pepper to bacon fat and cook until tender. Heat oysters in their liquid in saucepan until edges curl; remove oysters and reserve 2 cups of liquid. If there is not enough liquid, add enough chicken stock to make 2 cups.

Add rice, liquid and oysters to vegetable mixture in frying pan. Boil, stirring occasionally. Cover pot, lower heat, and continue to simmer until rice has absorbed liquid, about 15 minutes.

Serves 6 to 8 as part of a large meal.

in bacon fat. Add tomatoes and seasonings. Reduce heat. Simmer until okra is tender, about 20 minutes. Add chicken broth if mixture becomes too thick. Add crumbled bacon immediately before serving.

Serves 6 to 8 as part of a large meal.

FRIED CHICKEN

1 fryer chicken, cut into pieces
All-purpose flour
Salt and pepper
Vegetable oil, about 3 cups

SHRIMP PILAU

8 slices bacon
3 tablespoons butter
2 tablespoons chopped green pepper
1 tablespoon minced onion
2 cups water
1½ cups rice
3 teaspoons Worcestershire sauce
1 tablespoon flour
2 cups peeled and deveined shrimp
Salt and pepper to taste

Fry bacon until crisp and set aside. In steamer or pot with tight-fitting lid, mix water and 4 tablespoons of bacon grease. Add rice and cook.

In clean frying pan, melt butter. Sauté onion and green pepper for about 3 minutes. Sprinkle shrimp with Worcestershire and dredge with flour. Add shrimp to frying pan and sauté until flour is cooked and shrimp begin to turn pink. Season with salt and pepper. Add shrimp mixture to cooked rice and mix until rice is buttery. Add more butter if desired. Stir in crumbled bacon. Serve hot.

Serves 6 to 8 with large meal.

CORN PONE

1½ cups stone-ground yellow corn meal
1½ cups cold water
1 teaspoon salt
Vegetable oil

Stir together corn meal, cold water and salt. Mixture will thicken as it sits. Cover bottom of large, flat-bot-

tomed skillet with vegetable oil. When oil is hot, drop corn meal batter into oil by tablespoonfuls, spreading into silver-dollar-size circles. Fry until brown on both sides, about 5 minutes total.

Makes about 10 "pones."

SWEET POTATO PIE

1 9-inch deep-dish pie crust
1¼ cups sweet potatoes, cooked and mashed,
  strings removed (1 large or 2 small potatoes)
4 tablespoons butter
¾ cup light brown sugar
3 eggs
¾ cup evaporated milk
½ teaspoon salt
¼ teaspoon freshly grated nutmeg
¼ teaspoon ground cloves
½ teaspoon ground cinnamon
¼ cup bourbon or dark rum

Cream butter and sugar. Add the mashed sweet potatoes. Add eggs and milk. Beat well. Add seasonings and bourbon or rum. Bake at 375° about 40 minutes, until top is golden and eggs are set.

MRS. SULLIVAN'S BENNE WAFERS

1 pound light brown sugar
3 sticks butter
2 eggs
2 cups all-purpose flour
1 teaspoon baking powder
¼ teaspoon salt

Sweet Potato Pie and Benne Wafers

2 teaspoons vanilla

1½ cups toasted sesame seeds

To toast sesame seeds: Place seeds in single layer on cookie sheet. Place in 350-degree oven for about 5 minutes, watching carefully. They should just begin to lightly brown. Or, purchase already toasted seeds.

Cream first three ingredients. Sift flour, baking powder and salt. Add to butter mixture. Stir until combined. Add vanilla. Stir in sesame seeds. Drop by ½ teaspoon on wax paper on cookie sheet. Cook at 300°

until brown, about 14 minutes. Cookies must be very brown, but not burned on the edges. Important: Let cool completely on wax paper, then peel away from paper. Store in airtight container.

Makes about 12 dozen. Wafers freeze well.

ASIAN DINNER FUND-RAISER

Ellen Lew, who has been catering in Savannah since 1985, is a continental cook; she enjoys Italian, German and Jewish cooking, as well as preparing regional foods. But her first love is the cuisine of Asia. "My father was American-Chinese; my mother was born in China. I felt that Asian cooking was something important to preserve, and to share with others," she says. Her interest has taken her to Hong Kong, Singapore and Thailand for classes and apprenticeships, and she has shared her knowledge with an enthusiastic audience of Savannahians.

This dinner—auctioned by the Savannah Symphony and purchased by patrons who wanted to support a worthy cause and reap savory rewards as well—is nine courses that represent the best of Asia: Peking Duck from Northern China, veal/turkey dumplings from Shanghai and grilled lemon grass chicken Thai-style. Squirrel Fish is a specialty found only in China's Szechuan Province.

For this meal, pull out your best accessories in red, the oriental color for good luck.

MENU

•

BEEF POT STICKERS WITH RED
WINE VINEGAR DIPPING SAUCE

VEAL TURKEY SHANGHAI DUMPLINGS
WITH KOREAN HOT SAUCE

HOT AND SOUR SOUP

GRILLED LEMON GRASS CHICKEN
WITH THAI SPICY PEANUT SAUCE

STIR-FRY CHICKEN WITH SUGAR
SNAP PEAS AND RED PEPPER STRIPS

BEEF WITH ASPARAGUS AND
WATER CHESTNUTS

CLASSIC PEKING DUCK WITH PANCAKES,
ONION BRUSHES AND HOISIN SAUCE

SZECHUAN SQUIRREL FISH

GINGER ICE CREAM

ALMOND COOKIES

SUGGESTED BEVERAGES:
*Jasmine, Oolong or Lichee Tea or
California Gewurztraminer or Chardonnay*

BEEF POT STICKERS

1 to ½ cups bok choy, about 8 to 10 leaves, remove thick, tough stalky white part, wash and cut into 1-inch pieces
⅔ cup lean, uncooked ground beef

4 scallions, diced fine
½ teaspoon salt
½ teaspoon sugar
Fresh ginger, chopped fine, equivalent to 1 teaspoon
2 tablespoons soy sauce
2 teaspoon cornstarch
1 tablespoon sesame seed oil
1 package gyoza skins (from Asian food market)

Egg wash:
1 egg yolk mixed with
1 teaspoon water
1 cup vegetable oil
1 cup chicken broth, divided

Bring water to boil in large pot. Add bok choy, bring to boil, cook 2 minutes and drain. Run cold water over leaves to cool. Squeeze out as much water as possible, then chop into fine shreds with a knife.

Mix bok choy, ground beef, scallions, salt, sugar, ginger, soy sauce, cornstarch and sesame seed oil. Line cookie sheet with wax paper and dust with cornstarch.

Place 1 teaspoon filling in center of gyoza skin. Brush beaten egg wash on half of skin with pastry brush. Bring opposite side together to form semicircle. Seal sides. Place all pot stickers side by side on waxed paper.

Heat about ¼ cup oil in large, heavy iron skillet. When oil is medium hot, add pot stickers. Fry at medium high uncovered until both sides are golden, turning once.

Add ¼ cup chicken broth. Cover skillet and steam pot stickers until skins are translucent, about 2 minutes. Remove cover and continue cooking over medium-high heat until chicken broth cooks down and pot stickers are crispy and browned and stick to skillet slightly, about 6 to 8 minutes.

Repeat process until all are cooked. Serve warm with dipping sauce.

Makes 40 to 45, depending on number of gyoza skins in package.

RED WINE VINEGAR DIPPING SAUCE

¼ cup red wine vinegar
2 tablespoons soy sauce
2 teaspoons diced scallions
1 teaspoon fresh ginger, crushed and chopped fine

Combine all ingredients. Use as dipping sauce with pot stickers, eggrolls, spring rolls, summer rolls and Chinese dumplings.

VEAL TURKEY SHANGHAI DUMPLINGS

Nappa cabbage, 1 pound net weight, after picking
  through and cleaning
½ pound ground turkey, breast meat only
¼ pound ground veal
3 scallions, chopped fine
Fresh ginger, equivalent to 1 tablespoon, chopped fine
½ teaspoon sugar
2 tablespoons soy sauce
1 tablespoon dry sherry
1 tablespoon oriental sesame seed oil
2 tablespoons unseasoned bread crumbs
1 package or more round gyoza skins

Eggwash:
  1 egg yolk, mixed with 2 teaspoons water
  Oil for deep frying

Shred cabbage and place in bowl. Sprinkle 1 teaspoon salt on cabbage, mix and set aside 20 minutes. Rinse cabbage well with cold water. Squeeze out as much liquid as possible from cabbage.

Combine cabbage with meats, onion, ginger, sugar, soy, sherry, sesame oil and bread crumbs. Line cookie sheet or baking pan with waxed paper.

Place 1 tablespoon filling in center of gyoza skin. Moisten edges with eggwash and fold together to form a half circle. Place dumplings circle-side upwards on wax paper-lined baking sheet.

Steam dumplings for 10 minutes: Use steamer or large pot with cover, placing dumplings on plate and small bowl as pedestal in large pot. After 10 minutes, remove dumplings from steamer and set aside to cool and dry off. This may be done 24 hours prior to final preparation.

When ready to serve, heat oil in fryer or wok to 375°, just below smoking point. Place 8 to 10 dumplings in hot oil and fry until golden brown. Place on paper towels to drain. Will stay warm up to 30 minutes. Serve with Korean hot sauce.

Makes 40 to 50 appetizer servings.

Leftover gyoza skins can be frozen. Wrap well in plastic wrap, place in freezer bags and squeeze out air before freezing.

Korean Hot Sauce

3/4 cup Korean hot pepper paste or hot bean sauce
1/4 cup Japanese white rice or wine vinegar
1 teaspoon sugar
1 teaspoon toasted sesame seeds (optional)
1 teaspoon finely diced scallions (optional)

Blend first four ingredients together and sprinkle diced scallions on top. Serve with Shanghai dumplings.

Hot and Sour Soup

Marinade:
   1 teaspoon soy sauce
   1/4 teaspoon cornstarch
   1/2 teaspoon vegetable oil
   1 teaspoon dry sherry

1/2 pound lean pork, cut in strips 1/8 inch by 1 inch
8 cups chicken broth
6 Chinese mushrooms, soaked in hot water for
   45 minutes, stems removed, washed well and
   cut in julienne strips
2 tablespoons bamboo shoots, drained,
   julienne sliced with grain
8 ounces tofu, cut into strips
1 tablespoon dry sherry
2 tablespoons cornstarch, mixed with 1/4 cup water
2 eggs, beaten
2 tablespoons soy sauce
Salt to taste
6 tablespoons Japanese rice vinegar
2 teaspoons white pepper
1 tablespoon sesame seed oil
3 scallions, diced
3 slices boiled ham, julienned, matchstick size

Marinate pork strips in marinade for 10 minutes. Bring chicken broth to boil. Add pork, mushrooms, bamboo shoots, tofu and sherry. Return to boil. Stir in cornstarch and water mixture to slightly thicken soup. Turn heat low. Pour eggs in slow steady stream into soup, stirring the entire time to separate egg strands.

Add soy sauce and salt to taste. Mix vinegar and pepper and fold into soup. Add sesame seed oil. Ladle soup into tureen or individual bowls. Garnish with ham shreds and scallions.

Serves 8 to 10.

GRILLED LEMON GRASS CHICKEN

1 pound boneless skinless chicken breasts
8 pieces lemon grass, each 6 inches long
1 teaspoon lemon pepper
1 teaspoon salt
Juice from 2 fresh limes
3 tablespoons virgin olive oil
25 to 30 6- or 8-inch wooden skewers

Soak skewers in cold water for an hour before using.

Cut chicken into strips 3 inches long and 1 inch wide.

Make marinade of lemon pepper, salt, fresh lime juice and oil. Add chicken strips. Fold in lemon grass. Marinate for at least 6 hours, or overnight, in refrigerator in plastic bag.

Thread chicken strips onto skewers.

Spray grill with vegetable spray and heat. Place skewered chicken on grill to cook, turning several times during cooking process. When chicken is done, serve at once with Thai spicy peanut sauce.

Serves 6 to 8 as part of a Chinese meal.

THAI SPICY PEANUT SAUCE

½ cup chunky style peanut butter
⅓ cup chicken broth (heat to warm in microwave)
2 tablespoons soy sauce
Fresh ginger, equivalent to 1½ tablespoons
  chopped fine

1 tablespoon oriental sesame seed oil
½ to 1 teaspoon crushed red hot pepper flakes

Whisk all ingredients together until smooth. Serve at room temperature.

STIR-FRY CHICKEN WITH SUGAR SNAP PEAS AND RED PEPPER STRIPS

1 whole boneless, skinless chicken
  breast, sliced into 1½-by 1-inch strips
Fresh ginger, equivalent to 2
  tablespoons, crushed and chopped
1 clove garlic, peeled, crushed and minced
2 tablespoons soy sauce
2 tablespoons cornstarch
2 tablespoons dry sherry
1 pound fresh sugar snap peas, trimmed
1 red pepper, cored, cut into 1 x 2 inch strips
3 tablespoons vegetable oil, divided
½ cup or little more chicken broth
Salt and pepper to taste

Marinate chicken in ginger, garlic, soy sauce, cornstarch and sherry for 20 minutes.

Heat wok or skillet. Add 2 tablespoons oil and roll around to coat cooking surface of wok or skillet. When oil is hot, add chicken and stir-fry until cooked. If chicken sticks to cooking vessel, add a little more oil in area where chicken is sticking. Remove cooked chicken from wok and set aside in bowl. Quickly wash out wok or skillet if sticky. Place back on stove and heat. Heat remaining oil. When hot, add sugar snap peas and stir-fry quickly, 30 to 45 seconds. Add chicken broth and cooked chicken to sugar snaps. Stir until a smooth sauce mixture is achieved. Add more chicken broth if necessary. Season with salt and pepper to taste. Just before serving, fold in red pepper strips.

Serves 6 to 8 with rice as part of a Chinese dinner.

BEEF WITH ASPARAGUS AND WATER CHESTNUTS

1/2 pound flank steak, cut across grain into 1/8-inch
  strips
1 1/2 pounds fresh asparagus
2 tablespoons oil, divided
1 can sliced water chestnuts, drained
1/2 to 1 cup chicken broth, or hot water
Scallions, diced, or sprigs of parsley for garnishing

Marinade:
  1 tablespoon soy sauce
  1 teaspoon dry sherry
  1 clove garlic, minced
  1 small piece ginger, crushed
  1 teaspoon sugar
  1 tablespoon cornstarch

Marinate steak for at least an hour.

Wash and snap tough ends off asparagus. Cut diagonally into 1/4 inch slices. Heat pot of water large enough for asparagus and bring to boil. Put asparagus in boiling water and bring to boil again. Remove from heat and drain in colander. Set aside. Heat 1 tablespoon oil in wok. When hot, add marinated beef and stir-fry about 2 minutes, more if you prefer beef well-done. Add 1/2 to 1 cup of chicken broth or hot water; the amount will determined the thickness of the gravy.

Bring to boil and add sliced water chestnuts. Put asparagus back in wok and mix well with beef. Remove from wok and place on serving platter. Serve immediately. Garnish with diced scallions, and parsley sprigs, if desired.

Serves 6 to 8 as part of Chinese dinner.

CLASSIC PEKING DUCK

1 fresh duck (5 pounds or larger), cleaned, with
  head attached
2 quarts water
1/2 teaspoon baking soda

Coating:
  1 quart water
  3 tablespoons molasses
  2 tablespoons sherry
  2 tablespoons soy sauce

12 to 18 Mandarin pancakes (found in Asian markets)
8 onion brushes

Peking Sauce:
  2 tablespoons Hoisin sauce
  1/4 teaspoon sesame oil
  1/4 teaspoon sugar

Bring water and soda to a boil. Drop in duck, ladle water over, and blanch for about 30 seconds. Remove duck. Discard water.

For coating: Bring water and molasses, sherry and soy sauce to a boil in wok. Hold duck over wok and ladle coating syrup evenly over surface of duck. Repeat

shape. Garnish with onion brushes.

Brush warm pancakes with Peking Sauce. Add onion brushes and a few pieces of duck and skin. Roll up and eat.

SZECHUAN SQUIRREL FISH

1 whole fish, about 1¹/₂ to 2 pounds, cleaned
  and scaled (red snapper is a good choice)
Cornstarch
4 cups peanut oil

Sauce:
  4 dried chili peppers, chopped
  4 cloves garlic, coarsely chopped
  2 slices fresh ginger root, coarsely chopped
  1 tablespoon dark soy sauce
  2 tablespoons dry sherry
  1 tablespoon chili paste
  1 tablespoon bean sauce
  1 teaspoon Chinese or red wine
  1 teaspoon sugar
  1 tablespoon cornstarch, dissolved in ³/₄ cup cold
    chicken broth and 2 tablespoons sesame oil
  2 scallions, chopped, for garnish

about six times.

Hang duck in a cool place with circulating air (a fan works well) for at least 4 hours, until skin is dry to the touch.

To roast: Preheat oven to 375°. Place duck breast side up on rack of roasting pan. Cover with tent of aluminum foil (avoid touching skin.) Reduce temperature to 350° and roast for 30 minutes. Turn duck over, cover with foil and continuing roasting at 325° for 30 minutes longer. Turn duck back to breast side up and remove foil. Roast for 5 to 10 minutes more, or until skin is golden brown. Watch to see that duck does not burn.

To make onion brushes: Trim white ends of green onions into 2¹/₂-inch lengths. Make repeated cuts through both ends, leaving the center intact. Place onions in ice water and refrigerate. Ends will curl, forming the brushes.

To serve, transfer duck to cutting board. Remove skin in large pieces, cut meat in bite-size pieces and arrange on serving platter. Cover with skin pieces and position wings and legs properly, creating original

Slash skin of fish with sharp knife in pattern. With hands, pat on cornstarch rather thickly, coating all of fish.

Heat oil in wok to 375°. Place fish in hot oil, and spoon oil over fish until fish is completely cooked, about 15 minutes. When done (insert fork into flesh and see that juices run clear and texture appears right), remove fish carefully from oil and place on warm serving platter. Quickly make sauce.

To make sauce, sauté chili peppers, garlic and ginger root in a small amount of oil used to cook fish. When oil is flavored, about 1 minute, add rest of sauce ingredients, except scallions. Allow to thicken. Pour over hot fish. Garnish with scallions.

GINGER ICE CREAM

2 cups whole milk
2 cups whipping cream
5 slices fresh ginger, each about the size of a quarter
1 cup sugar
2 or 3 beaten egg yolks
2 tablespoons chopped Raffetto's stem ginger in syrup
3 tablespoons ginger syrup

Combine milk, cream and ginger slices; heat to just bubbling over low heat. When bubbles appear on edges, add sugar and stir well. When sugar is completely dissolved, whisk beaten egg yolks into mixture and whisk until incorporated within mixture. Keep cooking over low heat until egg yolks are thoroughly cooked, about 8 minutes.

Pour mixture into large glass or stainless steel bowl. Place plastic film over bowl and refrigerate for at least 6 hours.

When ready to make ice cream, remove ginger slices and add chopped stem ginger and ginger syrup. Place mixture in batches in blender or food processor and process until thoroughly mixed.

Make ice cream in usual manner by churn freezer or electric ice cream mixer. Makes 8 servings.

ALMOND COOKIES

1/2 cup butter, room temperature
1 1/2 cups powdered sugar
2 teaspoons baking soda
1/4 teaspoon baking powder
Pinch salt
1 teaspoon water
1 egg
1 teaspoon almond extract
2 1/4 cups all-purpose flour
25 almonds

Egg wash:
  1 egg yolk mixed with 1 teaspoon water

Cream together butter and sugar. Add baking soda, baking powder, salt, water, egg, almond extract and beat until well mixed. Add flour. Mix together with fork or fingers to form dough.

Pinch off dough and roll into about 25 balls. Place on lightly greased cookie sheet 2 inches apart. Flatten each dough ball with heel of hand. Place an almond in center or each cookie.

Brush egg wash lightly across cookie, almond and dough.

Bake almond cookies for 13 to 15 minutes in preheated 350-degree oven. Cookies should be a deep yellow when done. Do not overbake. Cool on rack. Store in tightly covered container with waxed paper between each layer of cookies.

A Wild Game Supper

Throughout Savannah's history, visitors to the area have been entertained with hunting trips to nearby plantations along the Savannah River. Hunting offered the thrill of the chase, a chance to show off the land, and, with luck and skill, yielded a provision colonists adored.

Today, in the South, hunting remains a family heritage. A modern hunter explains: "Hunting is a tradition in the Lowcountry that has often been passed from father to son or daughter. It is a way of life, and the traditions have survived to this day. There is something special about seeing the sun rise or set as you watch an incoming flight of ducks or a svelte deer creeping through the woods. The dawn breaks away from the darkness and in the stillness and the cool of the morning, life begins to erupt around you. With a friend or dog beside you, you watch and wait for the game to come.

"We have passed down much of the original flavor of Southern hunting through old recipes and new ones that we continue to create. Our non-hunting friends seem to enjoy eating the game, as well as the stories of 'the hunt.'"

This party for 20 takes place among good friends, all of whom have been told to dress casually and come with a preordained dish. The result is a showy, hearty spread that showcases the best the woods have to offer.

MENU
•

SAUTÉED QUAIL LEGS

SMOKED DOVE BREASTS WITH
PLUM SAUCE

First Course
QUAIL TERRINE WITH
GREEN MAYONNAISE

Buffet
GRILLED FILET OF DUCK BREAST WITH
ORANGE PORT WINE SAUCE

GRILLED VENISON TENDERLOIN WITH
MARCHAND DE VINS SAUCE

WILD RICE WITH PECANS

BUTTER SAUTÉED BRUSSELS SPROUTS

SALLY LUNN

Dessert Table
COLD PUMPKIN SOUFFLÉ

FRESH APPLE CAKE

SAUTÉED QUAIL LEGS

Quail legs, at least 2
 per person
Flour
Salt and pepper
1/4 cup butter, or more

Dust quail legs with flour. Season with salt and pepper. In heavy frying pan, melt butter until hot, but not smoking. Sauté legs on medium heat until golden brown. Watch carefully so as not to burn. Drain on paper towels. Add more butter if needed to sauté additional quail legs. Serve warm as an hors d'oeuvre with plum sauce for dipping.

Sautéed Quail Legs

SMOKED DOVE BREASTS

Juice of 1 lemon
1/4 cup butter, melted
1 teaspoon lemon pepper
1/2 cup Italian dressing
2 teaspoons Worcestershire sauce
12 dove breasts
12 strips of bacon

Mix first five ingredients together. Marinate dove for one hour. Wrap each dove with bacon. Spoon marinade mixture over and smoke according to your smoker's directions. Or, bake in 350-degree oven for 30 to 40 minutes. Juice should run clear when dove is punctured with toothpick. Cut dove into bite-sized pieces. Spear each with toothpicks. Serve on platter with plum sauce.

PLUM SAUCE

1 cup plum preserves or plum conserve
1 cup orange juice
Squirt of lemon juice

Simmer until thick. Serve warm as dip with quail legs and smoked doves.

QUAIL TERRINE

10 quail, legs removed, breasts boned
2 eggs, slightly beaten
1/2 teaspoon lemon pepper
1/2 teaspoon seasoned salt
1 cup grated Parmesan cheese
8 slices prosciutto
20 large fresh basil leaves
2 14 1/2-ounce cans artichoke hearts, drained
* and cut in half*

Line a loaf pan with parchment paper. Set aside. Remove quail legs. Refrigerate for later use. Bone quail breast. Discard bones and scraps or use for stock.

Beat eggs and seasonings together. Dip quail breasts and artichoke hearts into egg mixture and coat with Parmesan cheese.

In loaf pan, layer 1/2 of quail breasts, 1/2 of the prosciutto, 1/2 of the artichokes. Top with basil leaves. Repeat layers of quail and prosciutto, ending with artichoke hearts. Cover the top with parchment paper and weight the top with baking weights or a clean brick. Place loaf pan in a larger pan filled with 1 1/2 inches of water. Bake at 350° for 1 hour and 20 minutes. Cool completely at room temperature. Refrigerate loaf pan overnight. To serve, carefully remove terrine from pan and slice into servings, about ¼ to ½ inch thick.

Serve as a first course on a bed of radicchio with rings of yellow and red peppers and green mayonnaise.

Serves 8 to 10.

Green Mayonnaise

½ *clove garlic*
4 *tablespoons fresh dill* } *or ½ cup fresh dill,*
4 *tablespoons fresh chives* } *no chives*
the equivalent of one egg of pasteurized egg product
½ *teaspoon salt*
1 *teaspoon dry mustard*
2 *tablespoons wine vinegar*
1 *cup vegetable oil*

Place first 7 ingredients in processor. Purée for a second. Add oil in steady stream until emulsified. Note: Pasturized egg product replaces raw egg to reduce risk of salmonella.

GRILLED FILET OF DUCK BREAST

Begin with number of breasts needed. Large ducks (such as Mallard or Black) serve two people. Small ducks (such as Widgeon, Gadwall or Wood) serve 1. Wrap breasts with bacon strips and secure with toothpick. Two small filets may be wrapped with 1 slice bacon. Season with lots of cracked pepper. Do not salt.

Cook over moderately hot charcoal fire and sear each side about 1 minute. Continue to cook until bacon appears done—about 10 minutes. Do not overcook.

Duck should be juicy and pink when done. If overcooked, it will be dry and tough.

Salt to taste after cooking.

Orange Port Wine Sauce

1 *cup orange marmalade*
¼ *cup white port wine*
¼ *cup orange juice*
Zest of 2 oranges
2 *tablespoons lemon juice*

Combine first 4 ingredients in saucepan. Mix thoroughly, simmer a few minutes to reduce the liquid and thicken the sauce. Add lemon juice. Serve with game birds and wild rice.

Grilled Venison Tenderloin

1 *tenderloin of venison, well-trimmed*
2 *tablespoons soy sauce*
2 *tablespoons Kitchen Bouquet®*
2 *tablespoons Worcestershire sauce*

Combine ingredients. Marinate venison tenderloin several hours in marinade. Wrap well with bacon, securing with wooden toothpicks. Cook over hot grill for 10 minutes, turning to cook evenly.

Serves 8 to 10.

Marchand De Vins Sauce

4 *tablespoons butter*
6 *green onions, mostly green tops*
½ *teaspoon freshly ground pepper*
½ *teaspoon dried thyme*
¾ *cup good red table wine*
1 *pound fresh mushrooms*

½ cup flour
3 cups beef stock (preferably venison stock)
2 tablespoons sherry
2 tablespoons brandy
Salt to taste

Braise onions, pepper and thyme in butter. When limp, add red wine. Cook down a little. In a cup or small bowl, make a thick paste with flour and a little beef broth. Add this paste and rest of beef stock to wine mixture. Stir, add sliced mushrooms, sherry and brandy. Simmer until mushrooms are cooked to your pleasure and sauce is thick. If sauce needs to be thickened more, make a paste of red wine and flour and stir in and simmer.

Serve with venison tenderloin.

WILD RICE WITH PECANS

1 cup raw wild rice
¼ cup butter or margarine
2 cups chicken stock
¼ cup green onions, sliced
¼ cup chopped pecans, toasted

Wash wild rice well. In saucepan, melt butter. Sauté wild rice for a minute in butter. Add chicken stock. Bring rice to a boil, reduce heat to low and cook until rice is tender, about 45 minutes. Just before serving, stir in green onions and toasted pecans.

To toast pecans: Place chopped nuts in single layer on baking sheet. Toast in 350-degree oven for about 5 minutes, until they are beginning to brown, but do not burn.

Serves 8.

BUTTER SAUTÉED BRUSSELS SPROUTS

3 to 4 sprouts per person.

Wash brussels sprouts. With a knife, cut a ½-inch cross into the bottom of each sprout. Boil in salted water until just tender, about 7 minutes. Drain and refrigerate until ready to serve. When ready to serve, melt ½ cup butter per pound of sprouts in a large saucepan. Add brussels sprouts and toss in butter until they are warmed and coated.

SALLY LUNN

This sweet yeast bread was named for the 18th-century Englishwoman said to have first made it in Bath. It is most impressive baked in a Bundt pan, sliced and served to guests on a silver platter.

1 package dry yeast
1½ cups warm milk
3 eggs
3 tablespoons sugar
1½ teaspoons salt
5 cups flour
½ cup melted butter

Soften yeast in warm milk in large mixing bowl. In an electric mixer, combine yeast, eggs and sugar. Add salt and about 3 cups of flour. Stir in remaining flour by hand. Add butter and beat again. Batter will be thin. Let rise in mixing bowl until doubled in bulk, about 1 hour.

Beat down and pour into well-greased tube pan or bundt pan. Let rise again until doubled in bulk, about 1 hour. Bake at 350° for 45 minutes.

Serves 10 to 12.

COLD PUMPKIN SOUFFLÉ

6 egg yolks
3/4 cup dark brown sugar
1 1/4 cups hot milk
1 15-ounce can solid-pack pumpkin purée
1/2 teaspoon salt
1 teaspoon cinnamon
1/4 teaspoon ground ginger
1/4 teaspoon ground cloves
1/2 tablespoon unflavored gelatin, dissolved in 1/3
  cup dark rum or sherry
1/2 teaspoon vanilla extract
3/4 cup ginger or orange marmalade
6 egg whites, stiffly beaten with 1/2 cup sugar
3/4 cup heavy cream lightly whipped
1 bar of semi-sweet chocolate, shaved with a knife

Whisk egg yolks and brown sugar in heavy 3-quart pan until thick and pale yellow; whisk in hot milk slowly, then add pumpkin. Add seasonings. Stir over moderate heat until hot but not simmering. Mix in the dissolved gelatin and the marmalade. Place saucepan in a bowl of ice water and continue to stir until the mixture is cool, but not set.

Beat egg whites; fold gently into pumpkin mixture.

Place pumpkin soufflé in soufflé dish with paper collar. Cover and chill 6 hours or more.

To serve: Remove collar. Decorate dessert with whipped cream and chocolate shavings.

Serves 10 to 12.

FRESH APPLE CAKE

1 1/2 cups vegetable oil
2 cups sugar
3 eggs
3 cups flour
1 teaspoon salt
1 teaspoon baking soda
2 teaspoons vanilla
3 freshly chopped apples
1 cup chopped pecans

Filling:
  1/2 cup butter
  1/4 cup evaporated milk
  1 cup light brown sugar
  1 teaspoon vanilla extract

With electric mixer, combine oil and sugar until light and fluffy. Add slightly beaten eggs. Beat well. Sift together flour, salt and soda. Add flour mixture to oil mixture. Batter will be very thick. Add vanilla, chopped apples and pecans. Mix well by hand.

Pour batter into 11-x-15-inch baking pan. Bake at 350° for 30 minutes. Cool. Split cake in half. Pour filling over bottom layer, then top with second layer. Pour filling over top. Filling will run down sides, so you may keep spooning back over top and sides.

For filling, boil butter, milk and brown sugar over medium heat for 5 minutes. Add vanilla. Pour warm over layers.

For moister cake, make double recipe of filling. Cake is best made one day in advance so filling can seep into cake.

Serves 10 to 12.

THANKSGIVING FEAST

"Thanksgiving is Savannah's number-one holiday. It is a time when Savannah does home entertaining on a grand scale," explains one Savannah hostess. "The important thing is that Savannah cooks consider preparations for this meal a privilege, not a chore. Families enjoy whatever time off they have together and don't seem to mind doing whatever it takes to make this meal special and beautiful."

Pull out the best china and polish the silver for this elaborate buffet that begins with a spicy beverage for both children and adults, moves on to a soup course served at the table, proceeds to a groaning board of meats and side dishes and concludes with a bounty of sweet Southern traditions: a caramel layer cake, egg custard pies, brown sugar surprises and ambrosia. What a day for thanksgiving!

HOLIDAY BREW

1½ quarts cranberry juice
2 quarts apple juice
¼ cup brown sugar
3 cinnamon sticks
1 tablespoon whole cloves
Additional cinnamon sticks,
  if desired

MENU
•
HOLIDAY BREW
MRS. SULLIVAN'S CRISPY CHEESE WAFERS
RELISH TRAY
CRAB BISQUE THIRTY SEVENTH
FROZEN CRANBERRY SALAD
ROASTED TURKEY WITH GRAVY
BAKED HAM
CORNBREAD DRESSING
SCALLOPED OYSTERS
CORN SOUFFLÉ
SWEET POTATO SOUFFLÉ
HOLIDAY BEST BROCCOLI CASSEROLE
CLOVERLEAF ROLLS
EGG CUSTARD PIES
AMBROSIA
CARAMEL CREAM CAKE
BROWN SUGAR SURPRISES
SCOTTISH SHORTBREAD

Put brown sugar, cinnamon sticks and cloves in the upper basket of percolator. Put juices in bottom. Let mixture perk as if making coffee. Serve with cinnamon sticks as stirrers, if desired.

Makes 3½ quarts.

MRS. SULLIVAN'S CRISPY CHEESE WAFERS

1 cup butter, softened
2 cups extra sharp grated
  Cheddar cheese
2 cups flour
¼ teaspoon salt
½ teaspoon cayenne pepper
2 cups Rice Krispies®
½ cup chopped pecans
  (optional)

Combine butter and cheese. Sift flour, salt and red pepper. Blend into butter/cheese mixture. Stir in cereal and nuts, if using. Roll dough into small balls the size of marbles. Flatten with a small fork on ungreased, non-stick cookie sheets.

Bake at 350° for 11 minutes, or until lightly browned.

Yield: about 4 dozen. Wafers freeze well.

RELISH TRAY

Fill pretty glass divided tray with sweet and sour pickles, pickled peaches, black and green olives and any chuntneys or relishes your family likes.

CRAB BISQUE THIRTY SEVENTH*

6 tablespoons butter
1 cup green onion, roughly cut
1/2 cup celery, roughly cut
One 1-inch piece of carrot
6 tablespoons flour
2 1/2 cups milk
2 1/2 cups chicken broth, preferably homemade
1/4 teaspoon nutmeg
1/4 teaspoon white pepper
1/8 teaspoon cayenne pepper
1 cup cream
1/4 cup sherry
1 pound claw crab meat, picked through for shells

Melt butter over low heat in saucepan. Mince green onion, celery and carrot in food processor. Or, mince by hand. Add vegetables to butter and cover saucepan with lid. Over low heat, allow vegetables to "sweat," which removes rawness and develops flavor, about 5 minutes. Whisk in flour and cook for 2 minutes to remove starchy taste. Whisk in milk and broth. Bring to a boil, whisking occasionally.

Add seasonings, cream, sherry and crab. Serve immediately.

Serves 12.

*Recipe courtesy of Elizabeth on Thirty Seventh Restaurant.

FROZEN CRANBERRY SALAD

1 16-ounce can whole berry cranberry sauce
Juice of 1 lemon
1 cup whipping cream, whipped
1/4 cup mayonnaise
1/2 cup confectioners' sugar
1 3-ounce package cream cheese, softened
1 cup pecans, chopped (optional)

Combine cranberry sauce and lemon juice. Pour into mold sprayed with vegetable spray or into a square dish. Combine whipped cream, mayonnaise, sugar, cream cheese and nuts, if using. Spread this over cranberry layer. Freeze. Cut into squares or unmold on lettuce-lined plate.

Serves 12.

ROASTED TURKEY WITH GRAVY

1 12-14 pound turkey
Salt and pepper
2 cups chicken broth or 2 chicken bouillon cubes,
*   dissolved in 2 cups water*
¼ cup all-purpose flour

If turkey is frozen, defrost in refrigerator according to package directions.

Rinse turkey in cold water. Remove giblets. Dry with paper towels. Season inside and out with salt and pepper rather heavily.

In a shallow roaster, place 1 cup of water. Place turkey on roasting rack. Roast turkey, uncovered, in 325-degree oven for 3 to 3½ hours, until juices run clear and drumstick wiggles freely.

Remove turkey and place on platter to garnish.

To make gravy: Take a whisk to loosen all pan drippings in bottom of roaster. Strain into a glass measuring cup. Add flour to cold chicken broth, whisking until there are no lumps. Heat drippings. Add flour/chicken broth mixture to drippings, whisking constantly. Cook until thickened. Season to taste.

BAKED HAM

1 12- to 14-pound precooked ham

Bake ham at 325° for 2 to 2½ hours. Ham should be crisp on the outside, tender and juicy inside. If desired, brush ham with glaze of brown sugar and mustard or brown sugar and pineapple juice. Return to oven about 30 minutes more.

CORNBREAD DRESSING

¾ cup butter or margarine
1 cup chopped celery
¼ cup finely chopped onion
4 pieces of toast, crumbled
5 cups crumbled cornbread
2 teaspoons salt
1½ teaspoons pepper
1½ teaspoons poultry seasoning
3 cups turkey broth
4 eggs, beaten
1 pint oysters, drained and chopped (optional)

To make turkey broth: Place 1 quart of water in stockpot. Add turkey giblets removed from center of turkey during cleaning. Add 1 teaspoon salt and ½ teaspoon pepper. Bring to a boil, reduce heat and cook on medium heat for about 1 hour. Remove lid and cook 15 minutes more to reduce stock slightly and produce a richer broth. You should have 3 cups remaining.

Melt butter in heavy skillet. Sauté celery and onion. Put crumbled toast and corn bread in large bowl. Pour butter and vegetables over. Add seasonings, eggs and broth. Stir well. Add oysters, if using, and mix well.

Bake uncovered at 350° for about an hour, until set. Serve with turkey gravy.

Serves 12, with leftovers.

SCALLOPED OYSTERS

1 pint shucked oysters, washed and drained well
2 cups oyster cracker crumbs
1/4 cup melted butter
1/2 teaspoon salt
1/2 teaspoon pepper
1 cup half-and-half
2 teaspoons sherry
Dash Tabasco®
1 teaspoon Worcestershire sauce

Mix cracker crumbs and butter. Arrange a layer of half the buttered crumbs in dish. Layer oysters over crackers. Season with salt and pepper. Cover with remaining crumbs. Combine half-and-half, sherry (if using) and Tabasco® and Worcestershire. Pour over casserole.

Bake at 400° for about 20 minutes, or until liquid has been absorbed.

Serves small portions to 8 to 10.

CORN SOUFFLÉ

2 cups fresh corn kernels, removed from about
* 4-5 ears of corn*
1/4 cup all-purpose flour
1 teaspoon salt
1/4 teaspoon freshly ground black pepper
3 eggs, well-beaten
1 1/2 cups milk
3 tablespoons melted butter or margarine

Mix together corn, flour, salt and pepper. Whisk together eggs, milk and melted butter. Stir into corn. Pour into buttered 2-quart casserole. Place casserole in larger pan filled with hot water.

Bake at 350° for 50 minutes to 1 hour, until filling is set and top of casserole is browned.

Serves 8 to 10 on large buffet.

SWEET POTATO SOUFFLÉ

4 cups sweet potatoes, mashed
* (approximately 2 large potatoes)*
2 eggs
1 cup sugar
1/2 stick butter or margarine, melted
1 teaspoon vanilla
1 tablespoon orange juice

Topping:
* 1 cup brown sugar*
* 1/2 cup flour*
* 1 cup chopped pecans*
* 1 stick butter or margarine, melted*

Combine sweet potatoes, eggs, sugar, 1/2 stick butter or margarine, vanilla and orange juice. Pour into greased 3-quart casserole dish. Combine topping ingredients. Spread over potatoes. Cook at 350° for 30 minutes, until brown and bubbly.

Serves 10-12.

HOLIDAY BEST BROCCOLI CASSEROLE

*1 large onion, chopped and sautéed in small amount
of butter*
*2 10-ounce packages frozen chopped broccoli, thawed,
but not cooked*
2 cans cream of mushroom soup
8 ounces melted processed cheese spread, your choice
1/4 cup half-and-half
2 eggs, beaten
Ritz® crackers for topping
Melted butter

Heat soup and cheese spread together until cheese has
melted. Add half-and-half and beaten eggs. Combine
onion, broccoli and cheese sauce. Top with crushed
Ritz® crackers. Drizzle with melted butter.

Bake at 350° for 30 minutes, until casserole bubbles.

Serves 10-12.

CLOVERLEAF ROLLS

1 cup boiling water
1 cup butter, cut into chunks
1/2 cup sugar
2 teaspoons salt
3 envelopes yeast
1 cup warm water (110° to 115°)
1 teaspoon additional sugar
2 eggs, beaten
7 cups bread flour

Pour boiling water over butter in large mixing bowl.
Add sugar and salt and stir until sugar is dissolved. In
separate bowl, combine warm water, yeast and 1 teaspoon sugar. Allow yeast to foam, about 10 minutes.
Pour yeast mixture into butter mixture. Add eggs.
Blend well. Add flour, one cup at a time, until soft
dough has formed. A heavy-duty mixer with dough
hook is excellent for this. If using mixer, knead dough
until smooth and elastic, about 5 minutes. Or, knead by
hand about 10 minutes, until dough is smooth and elastic.

Place dough in greased bowl and turn to coat all
sides. Cover with clean tea towel. Allow to rise until
doubled in size, about an hour. Punch dough down.
Pinch off small pieces of dough and roll into balls about
the size of a marble. Place 3 balls in each cup of a large
muffin tin that has been sprayed with cooking spray.
Cover loosely and allow to rise until doubled in size,
about 1 hour. Bake at 325° for 20 minutes.

Yields 2½ to 3 dozen rolls. Freezes well.

EGG CUSTARD PIES

4 eggs
2/3 cup sugar
1½ cups milk
1 cup whipping cream
1 teaspoon vanilla flavoring
1/2 teaspoon salt
1/4 teaspoon grated nutmeg
2 baked 9-inch pie crusts, not deep-dish

Whisk together all ingredients and pour into baked pie
crusts. Bake at 350° for 30 to 35 minutes, until knife
inserted about 2 inches from edge comes out clean.

Makes 2 pies, producing 8 slices each.

CARAMEL CREAM CAKE

Cake Layers:
  2 sticks margarine or butter
  3 cups granulated sugar
  6 eggs
  2 2/3 cups all-purpose flour
  1/4 teaspoon baking soda
  1 teaspoon salt
  1 8-ounce carton sour cream
  1 tablespoon vanilla extract

Caramel Frosting:
  1/2 pound (2 sticks) butter
  2 cups light brown sugar
  1/2 cup evaporated milk
  1/2 teaspoon vanilla extract
  4 cups powdered sugar
  6-8 toasted whole pecans, for garnish

AMBROSIA

2 dozen juice oranges
1/2 cup sugar, or to taste
1 8-ounce can unsweetened pineapple tidbits (optional)
1 cup shredded coconut (optional)

Peel and section oranges, removing all membranes. Sweeten to taste. Add pineapple, with juice, and coconut, if using. Serve in glass bowl with dipping utensil.

Serves 12.

Note: People feel strongly about ambrosia. Some won't eat it with coconut; others feel it's not right without it. We always prepared two bowls to please both groups.

For cake: Have all ingredients at room temperature. Preheat oven to 350°. Spray 3 or 4 9-inch pans (depending on how thick you want your layers) with vegetable spray and dust with flour.

Cream margarine or butter until light and fluffy. Add sugar and continue to beat until very light. Add eggs, one at a time and beat well after each addition. Sift flour, baking soda and salt. Add about 3/4 of the flour mixture, then a little sour cream and combine thoroughly. Repeat, alternating flour and sour cream, beginning and ending with flour. Stir in flavoring. Pour batter into prepared pans, using three for thicker layers and four for thinner layers. Tap pans on counter top several times to remove air bubbles. Bake at 350° for 20 to 35 minutes, depending on thickness of layers. Do not overbake. Cake will pull away from sides of pan when done, or test with toothpick. Remove from oven onto cake racks when done. Cool 10 minutes. Remove carefully from pan. Frost between layers with Caramel Frosting. When cake is assembled, frost top and sides. Decorate with toasted whole pecans.

For frosting: Melt butter, add brown sugar and then milk. Cook 2 minutes over medium heat, stirring constantly. Remove from heat. Add vanilla and pour over powdered sugar. Beat until smooth. Let cool slightly. Frosts 3 to 4 layers. Frosting will harden when cooled.

To toast pecans: Place pecans on baking sheet. Toast in toaster oven on lowest setting.

Cake serves 16. Cake freezes well.

BROWN SUGAR SURPRISES

1 stick of butter or margarine
2 cups light brown sugar
2 eggs, beaten
1 cup flour
1 teaspoon baking powder
1 teaspoon vanilla
3/4 cup chopped nuts
1/2 to 3/4 cup chopped dates

Combine butter and brown sugar. Beat well. Add eggs. Beat until light and fluffy. Sift flour and baking powder. Add to butter mixture. Stir in vanilla, nuts and dates.

Pour into 9-x-13 inch pan. Bake 30 minutes in 300-degree oven. Let cool on rack. Cut into small squares. Freezes well.

SCOTTISH SHORTBREAD

1 cup butter, softened
3/4 cup powdered sugar
1/4 cup cornstarch
13/4 cups all-purpose flour

Cream butter and sugar. Sift cornstarch and flour. Stir into butter mixture. Press mixture into 9-inch square pan. Bake at 325° for 30 to 35 minutes, until lightly browned all over. Cut immediately into tiny squares, a little bigger than a postage stamp. (If you do not cut immediately, they will get too crisp and will break into pieces when you try to cut them).

Makes 36 small squares. Freezes well.

CHRISTMAS EVE BUFFET

In a city that dotes on its history, tour guides are quick to point out Savannah's religious roots. John Wesley, the father of Methodism, preached at Christ Episcopal Church and is credited with beginning the first Sunday School in the nation there. Two of the oldest black congregations in the United States still gather at First African Baptist Church and the First Bryan Baptist Church, both organized by slaves in the late 1700s. St. John's Episcopal Church was built in 1852-53, and its current parish house served as headquarters for General William Tecumseh Sherman during his occupation of the city in the winter of 1865. The Cathedral of St. John the Baptist, with its twin Gothic spires, could be seen by the young Flannery O'Connor, who grew up across the street. Woodrow Wilson married Ellen Axson, granddaughter of the pastor, in the manse of the Independent Presbyterian Church in 1885.

Candlelit Savannah churches, which number in the hundreds in the Savannah phonebook, are filled to capacity on Christmas Eve with church-goers who then return home for elegant meals with family and friends.

This gathering takes place in a grand, traditional home on Skidaway Island. The house, decorated with native foliage and family keepsakes, is as festive as the guests, requiring an equally impressive repast.

MENU
•

CHAMPAGNE WITH CASSIS

SALTED PECANS

CREAMED CRAB WITH SWISS TOPPING

Buffet
CRANBERRY SALAD MOLD

COUNTRY HAM WITH ANGEL BISCUITS

CHICKEN AND ARTICHOKE CASSEROLE

CHUTNEY RICE

STIR-FRIED BRUSSELS SPROUTS

SHERRY CREAM CAKE

GINGERBREAD COOKIES

CHAMPAGNE WITH CASSIS

1 bottle good quality champagne
1 cup cassis (black currant liqueur)
Strawberries or raspberries

Mix champagne and cassis in punch bowl. Fill champagne flutes. Garnish each drink with one strawberry or raspberry.

SALTED PECANS

2 tablespoons butter or margarine
1 pound pecan halves
1 teaspoon salt

Place pecans in large shallow pan with butter. Bake at 200° for 1 hour, stirring every 15 minutes. (Butter will melt after first 15 minutes; stir periodically to coat nuts.) Place toasted pecans on absorbent paper. Sprinkle evenly with salt. Store in airtight container. Can be frozen.

CREAMED CRAB WITH SWISS TOPPING

4 tablespoons butter
4 tablespoons flour
1 cup half-and-half
4 tablespoons sherry
1 pound white crab meat, picked through for shells
Salt and pepper to taste
1 cup grated Swiss cheese

Melt butter in small, heavy bottomed saucepan. Whisk in flour, combine well and allow to cook over low heat for about a minute. Slowly add cream, whisking constantly. Stir over low heat until mixture begins to thicken. Add sherry. Taste for seasonings. Gently fold in crab.

Spoon onto scallop shells or into ramekins. Top with grated Swiss cheese.

Refrigerate until ready to serve. Cook at 400° about 10 minutes, until cheese melts and begins to bubble and brown.

Serves 10 as appetizer.

CRANBERRY SALAD MOLD

1 cup ground raw cranberries
 (measure after grinding)
1 cup sugar
1 package unflavored gelatin, dissolved in small
 amount of water

Cranberry Salad Mold

1 package lemon gelatin
1 teaspoon grated orange rind
1 9-ounce can crushed pineapple
1/2 cup boiling water
1/4 cup orange juice
1/2 cup chopped celery
1/2 cup chopped pecans
Curly lettuce leaves, to garnish
Fresh orange slices, to garnish

Mix sugar and ground cranberries. Let stand overnight. Add gelatin to boiling water and dissolve. Cool. Add other ingredients. Pour into mold lightly greased with mayonnaise. To serve, allow to stand at room temperature 10 minutes. Unmold onto lettuce-lined plate and surround with orange slices, cut in half.

COUNTRY HAM

You can do your ham the old-fashioned way, or you can buy a ready-to-bake country ham, which has simple instructions included on the package. Slice thin. Serve in small yeast bakery biscuits or Angel Biscuits.

If preparing ham the traditional way, soak ham for 48 hours in large pan of cold water to cover. Change water twice. Place drained ham in large oval disposable aluminum roasting pan. Boil in large roaster set over two burners in 1 quart water, set at a simmer, for 18 to 20 minutes per pound. Allow ham to cool, remove from water, trim off skin and most of fat. Ham may be sliced and served, or glazed with brown sugar and mustard or molasses and reheated for 30 minutes in a 350-degree oven. Carve with a sharp knife into paper-thin slices cut at an angle. Ham stores well in refrigerator wrapped in foil. Or, freeze in freezer bags.

ANGEL BISCUITS

2 packages dry yeast
1/3 cup warm water (105°–110° degrees)
3 teaspoons sugar
1 cup vegetable oil
2 cups buttermilk
5 cups self-rising flour, sifted
Melted butter

Dissolve yeast in warm water. Add sugar. Allow yeast to foam, about 5 minutes. Add oil and buttermilk. Add flour. Stir until blended. Pat out on floured board to about 1/4-inch thickness. Cut out with biscuit cutter, or, drop by teaspoons onto ungreased baking pan. Brush with melted butter.

Can be refrigerated until ready to bake. Allow to stand at room temperature for 15 minutes before baking.

Bake at 425° for 12 to 15 minutes, or until lightly browned.

Yields: 5 dozen rolls. Can be frozen.

CHICKEN AND ARTICHOKE CASSEROLE

4 pounds chicken breasts
1 cup butter
1/2 cup flour
3 1/2 cups milk
4 ounces Swiss cheese
2 ounces grated Cheddar cheese
1 teaspoon salt
2 cloves garlic, crushed
1 teaspoon red pepper
8 ounces fresh mushrooms, sliced

2 14-ounce cans artichoke hearts, drained and
*   quartered*
Optional garnishes:
Watercress, red pepper strips, toasted almonds

Boil chicken until tender. Remove meat from bone and cut in bite-sized pieces. Melt butter in large heavy pot. Whisk in flour slowly, allow to cook a minute, add milk, continuing to stir. Allow to thicken slightly. Add cheeses and seasonings. Heat, continuing to stir, until cheese is melted and sauce is bubbly. (Sauce will not be thick.) Sauté mushrooms in 1 tablespoon butter. Add chicken, mushrooms and artichokes to sauce. Pour into large greased casserole.

Bake for 30 minutes at 350°. Garnish dish with large clump of watercress in center. Or, take red pepper strips and form a "flower" surrounding watercress in center. Toasted almonds can also be used to garnish.

Serves 10 to 12 as part of buffet. Casserole freezes well.

CHUTNEY RICE

1 cup chopped onion
2 tablespoons butter
3 teaspoons curry powder
2 cups white rice
1 cup golden raisins
4 cups chicken broth
1 4-ounce jar chutney

Sauté onions in butter until soft. Sprinkle curry powder over onions. Add white rice, continuing to stir-fry. Add raisins and broth. Bake, covered, in baking dish sprayed with vegetable spray at 375° for one hour. After baking,

wrap with foil and wrap dish in towel. Will keep warm for up to four hours. Heat chutney. Stir chutney into rice before serving.

Serves 10 to 12 as part of buffet.

STIR-FRIED BRUSSELS SPROUTS

2 quarts brussels sprouts
1/2 pound bacon, diced
1/2 cup diced pine nuts
3 green onions, finely minced
1/4 teaspoon ground nutmeg
Fresh ground pepper

Core sprouts. Shred in small batches in food processor. Fry bacon until crisp. Remove most of grease. Add pine nuts. Stir-fry in fat about 2 minutes. Add Brussels sprouts, green onions and nutmeg. Stir-fry over medium heat until cooked, but crisp, 6 to 8 minutes. Stir in bacon and pepper.

Can be slightly undercooked, refrigerated, and reheated just before serving.

Serves 10 to 12 as part of buffet.

SHERRY CREAM CAKE

1 10-inch angel food cake, torn into bite-sized pieces
1 envelope unflavored gelatin
1/2 cup water
5 large egg yolks
3/4 cup sugar, separated
3/4 cup dry sherry
2 cups whipped cream, separated
1 teaspoon vanilla

Toasted almond slivers and whole raspberries,
  to garnish

Dissolve gelatin in water. Beat egg yolks and ½ cup sugar until light-colored. Add sherry. Cook egg mixture in double boiler over moderate heat until it thickens enough to coat the back of a metal spoon. Whisk the gelatin into the warm custard. Stir until completely dissolved.

Whip 1 cup of cream until thickened. Add vanilla. Combine custard and whipped cream. Fold cake pieces into custard cream until all are coated. Pour into buttered 10-inch tube pan. Cover and refrigerate until set.

Unmold by wrapping pan with a warm towel for a few seconds. Ice cake with extra cup of whipped cream whipped until stiff with ¼ cup sugar. Decorate with toasted almond slivers and whole raspberries.

Serve with raspberry-strawberry purée.

RASPBERRY-STRAWBERRY PURÉE

1 10-ounce box frozen sweetened strawberries
1 10-ounce package frozen raspberries
Juice of 1 lemon

Purée in food processor or blender. Strain for seeds (time-consuming but necessary). Pass with dessert.

GINGERBREAD COOKIES

1 cup butter, softened
¾ cup light brown sugar
½ cup molasses
1 egg
3½ cups flour

1 teaspoon each:
  Salt
  Baking powder
  Ground ginger
  Ground allspice
  Ground cloves
  Cinnamon

In large bowl, beat butter, brown sugar and molasses until light and fluffy. Add egg and remaining ingredients and beat until well mixed. Shape dough into a ball, wrap in plastic wrap and chill until firm (at least 3 to 4 hours).

Preheat oven to 350°. Lightly grease cookie sheets. Cut dough in half. On floured surface, roll one-half of dough one-fourth-inch thick (keep remaining dough refrigerated). Cut as many cookies as possible; reserve trimmings. Carefully place cookies on cookie sheets. Decorate with raisins, if desired. Bake 12 minutes, or until edges of cookies are lightly browned. Remove cookies to wire racks to cool. Repeat with remaining dough and reroll trimmings. Decorate baked and cooled cookies with frosting, if desired.

Makes 12 to 14 large cookies. Can be frozen.

THE GALA WEDDING RECEPTION

A wedding offers Savannahians a chance to do what they do best—celebrate in style. Ballroom-sized tents are erected in the squares or on the lawn of a family plantation overlooking the Intracoastal Waterway. Weddings and receptions are also held inside historic antique-filled homes or among the paintings and sculptures of an art museum.

We feature here two weddings by two of Savannah's most sought-after caterers. The reception in the Telfair Museum of Art was a menu created by Susan Mason. The evening began with frozen vodka and a bar featuring raw oysters, caviar and cold salmon while hot and cold hors d'oeuvres were passed. Reception guests then retired to the downstairs sculpture gallery for a seated dinner of baked quail, wild rice, buttery shrimp, vegetables lightly splashed with vinaigrette and trays of delectable sweets. A marriage of good tastes.

Next we go to an outdoor wedding catered by Trish McLeod. This wedding took place in a field of blooming azaleas, magnolias and 150-year-old twisted live oaks. Symphonic music played in the foreground and a boat puttered by in the distance as the bride and groom exchanged vows under a chuppah, a wedding canopy, they designed themselves. The menu is rich with flavor and lush with color, contrasting beautifully with the pale colors of spring.

FROZEN VODKA

Into clean half-gallon paper cartons, place 1 liter vodka bottle with label peeled off.

Boil water (this keeps it clear). Cool. Pour water to top of carton. Place carton in freezer.

When water begins to freeze, add roses or tulips on stems, all around carton in any design you prefer. Place cartons back into freezer to completely freeze.

Right before serving, peel carton away from ice. Place frozen vodka bottles in silver punch bowl (This is basically decorative). Have additional bottles of vodka in buckets of crushed ice.

MENU

•

FROZEN VODKA

CUCUMBER SANDWICHES

OYSTERS ON THE HALF SHELL

CAVIAR BAR

CRAB BALLS

ORANGE QUAIL

WILD RICE CASSEROLE

BAKED SHRIMP

MARINATED VEGETABLES

TRAY OF SWEETS

WEDDING CAKE
(recipe not included)

CUCUMBER SANDWICHES

Peel English cucumbers. Slice thinly. Cut thin-sliced white bread into rounds. Spread bread with Hellman's® mayonnaise. Just before serving, place cucumber slices on bread rounds. Sprinkle with salt and pepper. Add a sliver of crisp-fried bacon, if desired. 1 cucumber yields about 40 slices.

CAVIAR BAR

Serve glass bowls of caviar with grated eggs, chopped white onion, cream cheese and butter, lemons and toast points.

To make toast points: Remove crusts from white bread and cut into four triangles. Bake at 200° until very dry. Will keep in plastic bags for a week.

OYSTERS ON THE HALF SHELL

Serve raw, shucked oysters in the half shells on beds of rock salt with lemon wedges and hot cocktail sauce. (See recipe on page 28).

CRAB BALLS

2 slices bread, crusts removed
1/3 cup milk
1 tablespoon mayonnaise
1 tablespoon Worcestershire sauce

Crab Balls

1 tablespoon fresh parsley, chopped fine
1 tablespoon baking soda
1 teaspoon Old Bay® seasoning
¼ teaspoon salt
1 egg, beaten
1 pound jumbo lump crab meat

Moisten bread crumbs with milk. Add additional ingredients. Shape into balls. Deep-fat fry. Refrigerate in plastic bags. When ready to serve, reheat in oven.

Serve with sauce made of 1 cup Hellman's® mayonnaise, ½ teaspoon tarragon and 1 tablespoon capers, with a little juice from capers.

Makes 30-35 crab balls.

ORANGE QUAIL

3 tablespoons butter
4 slices bacon, chopped
4 quail, cleaned

2 oranges, peeled and roughly chopped

1 garlic clove, crushed
1½ cups finely chopped shallots
1¼ cups hot chicken stock
Fresh thyme sprig or 1 teaspoon dry thyme
Salt and pepper
1 tablespoon brandy
Croutons, watercress and strips of orange rind

Melt 2 tablespoons butter in large casserole and sauté the bacon until slightly cooked. Add quail and cook on all sides until brown. Add chopped oranges, garlic, shallots, stock, thyme, salt and pepper. Cover and cook in oven at 350° 30 to 35 minutes, or until tender.

Transfer quail to warmed serving dish and keep hot while preparing sauce.

Skim off fat. Strain cooking liquid into saucepot. Add brandy, and boil rapidly until liquid has reduced and is slightly thick. Remove from heat. Whisk in additional 1 tablespoon butter. Pour sauce over the quail. Serve garnished with croutons, watercress and strips of orange rind.

Serves 4. For large parties, allow 1 quail per person.

WILD RICE CASSEROLE

Wild rice (consult package for number of servings)
Beef broth, in place of water in preparing wild rice
¼ cup each green, red and yellow peppers, chopped, per 2 cups cooked rice
¼ cup onions, chopped, per 2 cups cooked rice
½ cup mushrooms, sliced, per 2 cups cooked rice
2 tablespoons butter, divided

Salt and pepper to taste
1/2 cup whipping cream per 2 cups cooked rice

Soak wild rice in water for one hour. Drain. Prepare according to package directions, using beef broth in place of water. When first bringing rice to boil, boil hard for 5 minutes with lid held tightly on. Then reduce heat and cook until tender. This can be done the day before serving.

When ready to serve, sauté green, red and yellow peppers and onion in butter. In a separate pan, sauté sliced mushrooms in butter. Mix wild rice and vegetables, tossing lightly to blend. Add salt and pepper to taste. Spray a casserole with vegetable spray. Add wild rice. Pour whipping cream over top of rice. Do not stir. Wrap tightly in foil. Warm in 325-degree oven for 30 minutes. Toss gently before serving.

Allow 1/2 cup rice per serving.

BAKED SHRIMP

5 pounds large shrimp, peeled and deveined
2 bunches green onion, chopped
1/2 cup butter, melted
2 tablespoons bread crumbs

Place half of shrimp in large casserole sprayed with vegetable spray. Sprinkle half of onions over top. Pour over half of butter. Repeat layers, ending with butter. Sprinkle with breadcrumbs. Bake at 350° for 30 minutes.

Serves 10, or 12 to 15 as part of buffet.

MARINATED VEGETABLES

New potatoes, 2 per person
Asparagus, 4 to 6 spears per person
Tomatoes, 1/2 per person

Boil whole new potatoes in salted water until fork tender, about 20 minutes. Drain. Cook asparagus in boiling water for 2 to 4 minutes, then drain quickly. While new potatoes and asparagus are hot, sprinkle with any brand of Italian dressing. Serve new potatoes and asparagus with sliced fresh tomatoes at room temperature on platters. After they are arranged, drizzle with lemon vinaigrette (see page 66).

FILLING FOR LEMON TARTS

1/2 cup butter
1/2 cup lemon juice
1 1/2 cups sugar
5 eggs

Pre-cooked pastry shells, preferably homemade,
  but available in specialty section of supermarket

Melt butter. Add lemon juice and sugar. Beat eggs. Add slowly, stirring constantly, and cook over medium heat until thick. Refrigerate.

Just before serving, pour into pre-cooked pastry shells. Fills 40 to 50 shells.

CHEESECAKE COOKIES

Crust:
  1 cup flour
  1/4 cup packed brown sugar
  1 cup chopped pecans
  1/2 cup melted butter

Combine flour, sugar, pecans and butter. Press crust into 9-x-13-inch pan. Bake at 350° for 10 to 15 minutes, until lightly browned.

Filling:
  2 8-ounce packages softened cream cheese
  1 cup sugar
  1 teaspoon vanilla
  3 eggs

Combine filling ingredients. Beat well. Pour over crust. Bake at 325° for 20 minutes.

Chill. Cut into squares before serving. Decorate tops with fresh fruit, if desired. Makes 24 large or 48 small squares. Can be frozen.

PECAN TASSIES

Pastry:
  3 ounces softened cream cheese
  1/2 cup softened butter
  1 cup all-purpose flour
  1/4 tcaspoon salt

Filling:
  1 egg, beaten
  3/4 cup brown sugar
  2 tablespoons softened butter
  1/4 teaspoon salt
  1 teaspoon vanilla
  1 cup finely chopped pecans

Mix pastry ingredients until blended. Chill. Form pastry into 24 balls; press with hands into bottom and up sides of ungreased miniature muffin tins.

For filling, beat together all ingredients except pecans.

Sprinkle a few nuts in the bottom of each pastry shell. Pour filling over nuts, filling each tin 3/4 full.

Bake at 350° for 20 to 25 minutes, or until filling is set.

Cool slightly; remove from muffin tins by running knife around edges. Cool on wire racks. Store in tightly covered container.

Makes 24. Can be frozen.

THE OUTDOOR WEDDING

CHATHAM ARTILLERY PUNCH

Reprinted with permission from *Savannah Style—A Cookbook* by the *Junior League of Savannah*.

2 gallons tea (green tea—1 pound tea to 2 gallons water.
  Soak overnight in tin bucket and strain.)
Juice of 3 dozen lemons
5 pounds brown sugar
2 gallons Catawba wine
2 gallons Santa Cruz rum
1 gallon Hennessy
  (3-star) brandy
1 gallon dry gin
1 gallon rye whiskey
2 quarts cherries
2 quarts pineapple cubes
10 quarts champagne

Mix the tea with lemon juice, preferably in a cedar tub, then add brown sugar and liquors. Let this mixture "set" for at least 1 week, or preferably 2 weeks, in covered container.

After "setting period" and when ready to serve, pour over cake of ice. Never chill in refrigerator or used crushed ice. When this is done, add cherries, pineapple cubes and champagne, pouring in slowly and mixing with circular motion. The punch is now ready to serve.

Serves 200.

FRUIT TABLE
(Amounts suggested to make the round table look opulent)

1 dozen mangoes, ripe, soft to
  the touch, peeled and cubed
1 watermelon, cubed, seeded
2-3 honeydews, peeled, cubed
3-4 cantaloupes, peeled, cubed
4-5 pineapples, peeled, cubed
5 pounds grapes, left in
  bunches, washed
40 peaches, cut at the last
  minute and tossed in
  pineapple juice
1 flat strawberries, washed
  but not hulled

Chocolate dip: Melt 3 8-ounce packages semi-sweet baking chocolate and thin with a little heavy cream, starting with 1/4 cup. Keep warm. Makes 3 cups. Caramel dip: Melt 1 bag caramel candies and thin with a little heavy cream, starting with 1/4 cup. Keep warm. Makes 3 cups.

MENU

•

CHATHAM ARTILLERY PUNCH

FRESH FRUIT TABLE WITH DIPS

FRESH VEGETABLE TABLE
WITH HERB CURRY DIP

PESTO BRIE AND
SUN-DRIED TOMATOES

POACHED SALMON WITH
CUCUMBER DILL SAUCE

TOMATO TARTS

CRAB REMOULADE

ARTICHOKE CHEESE DIP

CAJUN CHICKEN BITES
WITH JALAPEÑO MAYONNAISE

SNOW PEAS OR SUGAR
SNAPS WITH BOURSIN

HERB CURRY DIP

1 cup mayonnaise
¹/₂ cup sour cream
1 tablespoon each:
  Grated onion,
  Chopped fresh chives,
  Capers,
¹/₂ tablespoon lemon juice
¹/₄ cup fresh parsley
¹/₄ teaspoon paprika
¹/₄ teaspoon curry powder
2-3 shakes Worcestershire sauce
Garlic powder to taste (about ¹/₄ teaspoon)

Mix together. Makes about 1 ¹/₄ cups to serve about 30. Make 5 recipes for party of 200.

VEGETABLE TABLE

6 cans baby cocktail corn, available in large
  supermarkets and oriental markets
500 sugar snap peas
1 case asparagus, blanched briefly (1¹/₂ to 2 stalks
  per guest)
5-6 bags baby carrots, raw
2 heads cauliflower, raw, broken into bite-size pieces
2-3 bunches celery, peeled and cut in uniform sticks
200 new potatoes, cooked until tender, but not peeled
3-4 heads broccoli, raw, broken into bite-size pieces
7-8 English cucumbers, peeled, cut into uniform sticks

Note: To blanch sugar snap peas, place peas in colander and pour boiling water over them. (Placing peas in water will overcook them.) Asparagus can be placed in rapidly boiling water for 2 to 4 minutes, depending on desired tenderness. Drain and place immediately in ice water.

PESTO BRIE WITH SUN-DRIED TOMATOES

8-inch brie round, top rind trimmed away
Pesto:
  2 cups greens—any ratio of basil and parsley
    that you like; start with 1¹/₄ cups basil
    and ³/₄ cup parsley
  ¹/₂ cup pine nuts, walnuts or pecans
  ¹/₄ cup olive oil
  3 cloves garlic, peeled
  Fresh grated Parmesan cheese, about 1 cup

Process garlic, basil, parsley and nuts. Add olive oil in stream to facilitate processing and bind. Add more oil if needed. Add Parmesan. Freezes well.

Pesto Brie with Sun-Dried Tomatoes

SUN-DRIED TOMATOES

Tomatoes, peeled and sliced about ¹/₃-inch thick
Salt to taste

Dry tomatoes in dehydrator until desired dryness, about 9 hours for 8 stacks. Or, dry in 200-degree oven for about 4 hours. Tomatoes will be slightly chewy and not too dry. Store in baggies in freezer. Reconstitute them over low heat with olive oil, garlic and water or wine. Cook until they plump up and most of liquid is evaporated. The tomato slices should still be recognizable, as opposed to becoming a sauce. Slice tomatoes into slivers.

To assemble: Allow brie to come to room temperature or heat briefly in microwave. Spread pesto to cover top of brie. Decorate with tomato slivers. Serve with crackers or pita chips.

POACHED SALMON

1 8-9 pound salmon

Have fish market skin and fillet salmon, returning all bones, head, tail and skin.

Fish fillets will need to be checked for bones. Remove with tweezers. Trim fillets of fatty flesh. Wash fish and pat dry. Salt the fillets and match them back together, one on top of the other. Place skin on each side and wrap with cheesecloth and tie.

In a fish poacher or large roaster with lid, make a broth with bones, one large peeled yellow onion (quartered), 3 stalks celery and 3 peeled carrots. Salt broth to taste. Add 2 bay leaves. White wine can be added to water if desired. Cook broth for about 45 minutes. Remove vegetables or push to the side when placing fish in broth. Broth should cover or almost cover fish.

Poach fish in simmering broth for about 20 minutes, then turn fish over and continue cooking for about 20 minutes. Lid should be partially on. When cooked, remove fish to a cookie sheet, let cool and remove all accumulated liquid. Refrigerate for a few hours or overnight. Steam head and tail for about 8 to 10 minutes. Chill with fish.

Unwrap salmon. Using a small, sharp knife, scrape away dark flesh from outer sides of salmon. Place fish on platter or tray, garnished with large leaves such as cabbage, collards, banana or fatsia. Leaves should be well-washed, dried and sprayed with vegetable cooking spray. Use paper towel to distribute spray evenly and to remove excess oil.

Place head and tail at appropriate ends. Decorate fish with thin slices of one unpeeled English cucumber or lemon or lime slices.

Fill space around neck and base of tail with parsley. Decorate with flowers or cranberries speared with toothpicks.

Serve with sour cream, capers, chopped Vidalia onions and lemon wedges or with a cucumber dill sauce.

Serves 60 to 75 at cocktail buffet. Serves 20 for dinner.

CUCUMBER DILL SAUCE

1 English cucumber, peeled, grated and drained for about 1 hour

Mix with:
1 cup sour cream
1 cup mayonnaise
3 teaspoons mustard
3 teaspoons lemon juice
2/3 cup fresh dill, chopped
Salt and pepper to taste

Keep refrigerated. Make 4 recipes for party of 200.

TOMATO TARTS

1 sheet Pepperidge Farm® Puff Pastry, cut into small rounds
4 or 5 Italian plum tomatoes, cut into 1/4-inch slices (be sure to match pastry cutter to size of tomatoes)
1/2 cup white Canadian Cheddar cheese, grated
Salt and freshly ground black pepper, to taste
Fresh thyme leaves to flavor, chopped fine
Fresh grated Parmesan cheese
Olive oil

Prick pastry with fork. Brush pastry lightly with olive oil. Top with small amount of white Cheddar, then sprinkle with salt, black pepper and thyme leaves. Place one tomato slice on top of each round. Sprinkle lightly with Parmesan cheese.

Bake at 375° for about 15 minutes.

1 sheet of puff pastry makes 30 tarts.

CRAB REMOULADE

5 pounds white crabmeat
2 cups mayonnaise
2 tablespoons Dijon style mustard
2 teaspoons lemon juice
2 cloves garlic
2 tablespoons capers
4-6 tablespoons parsley
2 hard-boiled eggs
2 teaspoons dried dill
2-3 green onions, white and green parts
White pepper and Cayenne, to taste

Blend all ingredients except crab in food processor or blender until it forms a smooth sauce. Mix sauce gently with crab. Place into mold sprayed with vegetable spray. Chill until firm. Unmold and decorate with fresh herbs or flowers. Serve with Bremer® Wafers.

Serves 200.

ARTICHOKE CHEESE DIP

12 ounces marinated artichoke hearts,
  drained and chopped coarsely
1/2 cup each, mayonnaise and sour cream

Artichoke Cheese Dip on Crackers

1/2 cup grated Parmesan, Romano or Asiago cheese
3 tablespoons fresh tarragon or thyme
  leaves or 1 tablespoons dried

Combine all ingredients. Decorate with paprika and parsley. Bake at 350° for about 30 minutes. Serve with small stone-wheat thin crackers, breads or fresh vegetables.

Serves 30 to 35.

Brush boneless, skinless chicken breasts with a little olive oil. Sprinkle with desired amount of cajun spices. Grill on both sides until cooked through, about 10 minutes per side. Cut into cubes, chill. Before serving, bring to room temperature or warm slightly.

Serve with Jalapeño Mayonnaise.

Allow 1 chicken breast per 2 people.

JALAPEÑO MAYONNAISE

1 cup homemade or commercial mayonnaise
¼ teaspoon Cayenne pepper
¼ teaspoon chili powder
10 slices pickled jalapeño pepper, chopped finely
* or 1 fresh seeded jalapeño, chopped finely*

Mix together. Serve with chicken.
Make 4 recipes to serve to party of 200.

CAJUN CHICKEN BITES

Make your own cajun spices, or try a commercial blend:

CAJUN SPICES

2 parts each:
* paprika*
* white pepper*
1 part each:
* dried oregano leaves*
* dried basil leaves*
* chili powder*
* ground cumin*
* garlic powder*
* onion powder*
* salt*
* Cayenne pepper to taste*

SNOW PEAS OR SUGAR SNAPS WITH BOURSIN

To blanch snow peas: Place snow peas in boiling water and remove immediately to ice water bath. Toss and remove immediately to drain. Cut leaves open lengthwise, piping boursin inside. Or, leave whole if boursin is to be piped on top.

To blanch sugar snap peas, pour hot water over them while tossing. Cool and drain on paper towels. Do not immerse sugar snaps in hot water; they overcook too easily. Split sugar snaps or keep whole.

Prepare 200 pieces for party of 200.

Snow Peas or Sugar Peas with Boursin

BOURSIN

4 ounces butter, softened
8 ounces cream cheese, softened
1 small garlic clove, minced
1/4 teaspoon each:
  oregano, dried
  basil, dried
  dill weed
  dried marjoram
  dried thyme
  black pepper

Mix. Makes about 1½ cups. Will fill 200 snow peas or sugar snaps.

HOW TO MAKE A SMUDGE POT

Fill clay pots half-way with wet, not soaking, newspapers. Place damp Spanish moss on top. When guests begin to arrive, light the moss with dry newspapers. The smoke will deter the bugs. Place pots about every 10 to 12 feet around perimeter of the party.

CREDITS

The photography in *Savannah Entertains* is greatly enhanced by the glorious settings, fine furniture and lovely appointments we were privileged to use as props. My sincere "thank you" to the following people, listed alphabetically, who allowed us to photograph on their property:

Dr. and Mrs. John Angell—Ribs at Beaulieu
Dr. and Mrs. Leon Aronson—Asian Dinner Fund-raiser
Dr. and Mrs. Roy Baker—Thanksgiving Feast
Mr. and Mrs. Craig Barrow III—Plantation Brunch
Dr. and Mrs. Edward F. Downing—A Formal Fish Dinner
Mr. and Mrs. Jim Grable—July 4th Fish Fry
Mr. and Mrs. Howard Hackney—In the Spirit of St.
    Patrick's Day
Mr. and Mrs. Ronald Kronowitz—Best of Bailee's
    Jewish Cooking
Dr. and Mrs. Joseph V. Morrison Jr.—A Wild Game Supper
Mr. and Mrs. Rod McLeod—The Lowcountry Boil
Mr. and Mrs. Thomas A. Nash Jr.—Christmas Eve Buffet
Dr. and Mrs. David Ostman—Savory Summer Meal
Mrs. Mitchell Palles—Curried Shrimp Ladies' Lunch
Mr. and Mrs. Dennis Ronning—July 4th Fish Fry
Dr. and Mrs. Andy Sheils—Supper at Sea
Mr. and Mrs. Michael Terry—Elizabeth Terry's Tybee
    Porch Supper
Mr. and Mrs. Charles F. VandenBulck—The Outdoor
    Wedding Reception
Mr. and Mrs. Herb Wardell—July 4th Fish Fry
Mrs. L.H. Wilkes—New Year's Day Good Luck Meal
Also to:
Mr. and Mrs. Martin Karp for allowing us to photograph The Gala Wedding Reception at the Telfair Art Museum

We are also grateful to have been allowed to photograph in the following locations:
The Beach Institute African-American Cultural
    Center—A Gullah Board Meeting Buffet
Fort Jackson—The Oyster Roast
45 South Restaurant—An Elegant Evening
Forsyth Park—Symphony-in-the-Park Picnic
Telfair Museum of Art—An Elegant Evening,
    The Gala Wedding Reception

Although I do not consider myself a great cook, I am shamefully good at asking great cooks for their recipes and techniques. Savannah hosts, hostesses and caterers are always willing to share, and that willingness means that this cookbook contains some prized recipes never before seen in print. I have tried to credit as many recipes as possible in a separate listing that follows. Some special people, however, went beyond sharing recipes and actually cooked for our parties as well. Special thanks to:

Ashby Angell, her son, Charlie, and his wife, Laura, who prepared all the elements for the Ribs at Beaulieu meal;
Chef Walter Dasher, who prepared the dishes at 45 South Restaurant for An Elegant Evening menu;
The staff at Fort Jackson, who smoked oysters for The Oyster Roast;
Sally Giddens, who assisted her aunt Martha Nesbit in testing the Asian dishes;
Howard and Pat Hackney, Tom and Jane Philbrick and Russell and Cindy Jacobs, who contributed to the St. Patrick's Day meal;
Bailee Kronowitz, who planned and prepared the food for the Best of Bailee's Jewish Cooking menu;
Caterer Ellen Lew, who orchestrated and cooked for the Asian Dinner Fund-raiser;
Caterer Susan Mason, for allowing us to photograph at a wedding reception at the Telfair Art Museum, and then shared the recipes;
Caterer Trish McLeod, who cooked and provided recipes for The Outdoor Wedding Reception, as well as for the Lowcountry Boil at her home;
Liz Palles, who cooked for the Curried Shrimp Ladies' Lunch at her home;

Jim and Karen Pannell, Jerry and Margaret Miller, Dennis and Patty Ronning, Howard and Pat Hackney, Joe and Joann Morrison, Michael and Carolyn Donovan, Frank and Huldah Carlton and Bob and T. Gongaware, all of whom contributed items to the Wild Game Dinner at the Morrison home;

Karen Payne, who cooked for both the Symphony-in-the-Park Picnic and the Savory Summer Meal;

Restaurateur Elizabeth Terry, chef and owner of Elizabeth on 37th, who prepared the food for her Tybee Porch Supper;

Mrs. L.H. Wilkes and her grandson-in-law, Ronnie Thompson, who prepared the food for the New Year's Day Good Luck Meal.

Recipes—old and new—are the essence of this collection. I give credit to the following for offering to share old stand-bys and new discoveries:

Cathy Adler:	Carrot Ginger Soup
Ashby Angell:	Marinated Grilled Vegetables with Pasta and Pesto, Cole Slaw with Vinaigrette, Olive Country Bread With Rosemary
Charlie Angell:	Barbecued Ribs
Laura Angell:	Apple Pie with Crumb Topping
Val Bowers:	Egg Custard Pies
Marilyn Buck:	Horseradish Potato Salad
Susan Carter:	Gingerbread Cookies
Alva Compton:	Green Bean Bundles
Walter Dasher:	Crispy Scallops and Leeks With Burgundy Butter, Caesar Salad with Pesto Croutons, Grilled Veal Chops, French Green Beans, Horseradish Mashed Potatoes, Sherried Wild Mushrooms, Cinnamon Almond Shortbread Cookies with Fresh Seasonal Fruits and Raspberry and Mango Coulis
Dixie Crystals Sugar:	Caramel Cream Cake
Renée R. Dunn:	Boursin
Suzie and J.C. Fitzgerald:	Pesto and Tomato Terrine
Clara Eschmann:	Peach Ice Cream

Sarah Gaede:	Mint Juleps, Country Ham, Angel Biscuits
Alice Jo Giddens:	Lemon Squares, Fried Chicken
Pat and Howard Hackney:	Spinach Apple Salad, Mr. Roberts' Irish Stew with Shamrock Toast
Cindy Jacobs:	Whipped Leprechauns
Richard Johnson:	Richard's Barbecue Sauce
Bailee Kronowitz:	Chopped Chicken Liver, Beef Brisket, Whole Stuffed Baked Fish, Potato Latkes, Vegetable Mousse, Brioche or Challah, Georgia Pecan Clusters
The late Mary Lane: (Martha's grandmother)	Cornbread Dressing
Ellen Lew:	Beef Pot Stickers, Veal/Turkey Shanghai Dumplings, Grilled Lemon Grass Chicken, Hot and Sour Soup, Peking Duck, Szechuan Squirrel Fish, Stir-fry Chicken with Sugar Snap Peas and Red Pepper Strips, Beef With Asparagus and Water Chestnuts, Ginger Ice Cream, Almond Cookies
Susan Mason:	Frozen Vodka, Caviar Bar, Oysters on the Half Shell, Crab Balls, Cucumber Sandwiches, Orange Quail, Wild Rice Casserole, Baked Shrimp, Marinated Vegetables, Filling for Lemon Tarts, Cheesecake Cookies, Pecan Tassies, Chicken and Artichoke Casserole, Chutney Rice, Stir-fried Brussels Sprouts
Nellie McGowan:	Cream Cheese Poundcake
Trish McLeod:	Burma Bomb, Boiled Crab, Crudités with Herb Dip, Lowcountry Boil, Grilled Mustard Chicken, Pasta with Parsley-basil Pesto, Red Rice, Green Salad with Lemon Vinaigrette, Fruit Table with Caramel and Chocolate Dipping Sauces, Fresh Vegetable Table with Herb Curry Dip, Snow Peas or Sugar Snap Peas with Boursin, Poached Salmon, Brie with

Margaret Miller: Peso and Sun-dried Tomatoes, Tomato Tarts, Artichoke Cheese Dip, Chicken Bites with Jalapeño Mayonnaise, Crab Remoulade, "How To Make a Smudge Pot" Wild Rice with Pecans, Butter-sautéed Brussels Sprouts

Joann Morrison: Sautéed Quail Legs, Smoked Dove Breasts with Plum Sauce, Quail Terrine with Green Mayonnaise, Grilled Filet of Duck Breast with Orange Port Wine Sauce, Grilled Venison Tenderloin with Marchand de vins Sauce, Sally Lunn

Tom Nash: Champagne with Cassis

Luginia Neal: Breakfast Yeast Ring

Mona Nesbit: Scottish Shortbread

Liz Palles: Fresh Fruit with Boiled Dressing, Tomato Aspic, Shrimp Curry, Rice Ring, Brittle Bread, Charlotte Russe, Lace Cookies, Oven-roasted Garlic Potatoes, Cheese Biscuits

Karen Payne: Herbed Cream Cheese, Broccoli Salad with Sweet and Sour Dressing

Jane Philbrick: Champagne Midoris, Party Reubens, Cheddar and Rosemary Soda Muffins, Irish Coffee

Kacey Ratterree: Kacey's Cheese Biscuits

Patty Ronning: Fresh Apple Cake, Blueberry Crumble, Cornbread Muffins, Cranberry Salad Mold, Traditional Peach Cobbler, Sweet Potato Soufflé, Spicy Ham Loaf with Horseradish Cream, Molded Crabmeat Ring, Tomato Herb Muffins

Ann Sheils:

Sally Sullivan: Mrs. Sullivan's Benne Wafers, Mrs. Sullivan's Crispy Cheese Wafers, Brown Sugar Surprises

Elizabeth Terry: Green Herb and Goat Cheese Dip with Green Vegetables, Pickled Shrimp and Vidalia Onion, Chicken and Black-eyed Pea Salad with Honey and Mustard Dressing, Pepper-pecan Brioche, Ginger

Poached Peaches with Lemon Sherbet and Gingersnaps, Crab Bisque Thirty-Seventh

Eloise Wardell: Eloise's Tartar Sauce, Hush Puppies

Herb Wardell: Herb's Bloody Marys

Mrs. L.H. Wilkes: Turnip Greens, Roast Pork, Pecan Pie

Many recipes were developed and/or refined by Martha Nesbit specifically for this book. They include:

Cold Pumpkin Soufflé
Creamed Crab with Swiss Topping
Boiled Peanuts
Lemon Meringue Pie
Spicy Deviled Crab
Okra and Tomatoes
Shrimp Pilau (adapted from Lysa McCullough's recipe)
Oyster Pilau
Corn Pone
Sweet Potato Pie
Chocolate Bark
Chili
Brunswick Stew
Savannah Pralines
Tomato Pie (adapted from Trish McLeod's recipe)
Shrimp and Grits
Oysters with Green Sauce
Pan-fried Flounder
Pecan-coated Grouper
Asparagus with Lemon Butter
Frozen Cranberry Salad
Scalloped Oysters
Corn Soufflé
Holiday Best Broccoli Casserole
Cloverleaf Rolls
Ambrosia
Shrimp Paste
Vidalia-onion Vichyssoise
Crab Cakes with Dill Sauce
Stir-fry Vegetables
Sausage-stuffed Vidalia Onions (adapted from Elizabeth Terry's recipe)

BIBLIOGRAPHY

Creating this cookbook was made much easier because of the published works of other authors. Books used for reference and inspiration include:

Anderson, Jean and Elaine Hanna. *The New Doubleday Cookbook*. New York: Doubleday, 1985.

Berendt, John. *Midnight in the Garden of Good and Evil*. New York: Random House, 1994.

Child, Julia. *The Way To Cook*. New York: Alfred A. Knopf, 1989.

Coleman, Feay Shellman. *Nostrums for Fashionable Entertainments—Dining in Georgia*, 1800-1850. Savannah: Telfair Art Museum, 1992.

Dupree, Nathalie. *Southern Memories*. New York: Clarkson Potter, 1993.

Fowler, Damon Lee. *Classical Southern Cooking*. New York: Crown Publishers, Inc. 1995.

Gaede, Sarah. *Sarah Tells All*, cookbook self-published in Savannah in 1991.

Horn, Jane: editor. *Cooking A to Z*. California: Ortho Books, 1988.

Neal, Bill. *Bill Neal's Southern Cooking*. Chapel Hill: The University of North Carolina Press, 1985.

Nesbit, Martha Giddens. *Savannah, Crown of the Colonial Coast*. Memphis: Towery Publishing, 1992.

Junior League of Savannah. *Savannah Style, A Cookbook by the Junior League of Savannah, Inc.* Wimmer Brothers, 1980. Reprinted in 1996 by Favorite Recipes Press.

Taylor, John Martin. *Hoppin' John's Lowcountry Cooking*. New York: Bantam Books, 1992.

Wilkes, Mrs. L.H. *Famous Recipes From Mrs. Wilkes' Boarding House in Historic Savannah*. Self-Published in 1976, revised 1984.

Williams, Chuck and Joyce Goldstein. *Festive Occasions Cookbook*. San Francisco: Weldon Owen Inc., 1993.

INDEX